PRIMARY LANGUAGE LESSONS
Teacher's Guide

◆

Catherine Andrews

B.A. English Education, National Board Certified, Teacher of English, Hayesville Middle School, Hayesville, North Carolina

Mary Jane Newcomer

B.A. English Education, Teacher of English, Frostproof Middle-Senior High School, Frostproof, Florida

D1663086

Lost Classics
Book Company

Lake Wales, Florida

PUBLISHER'S NOTE

Recognizing the need to return to more traditional principles in education, Lost Classics Book Company is republishing forgotten late 19th and early 20th century literature and textbooks to aid parents and teachers in the education of children.

This guide is designed to accompany *Primary Language Lessons,* which was reprinted from the 1911 copyright edition. The guide contains all the original questions and exercises from the textbook along with suggested answers. It also includes new "Extended Activities" that reinforce and enhance the original study sections. In most cases, items that appear in the textbook for dictation lessons are not repeated in the guide for the sake of brevity, in an effort to produce a more affordable guide for the parent and teacher.

There have been multiple printings of this grammar text, and while we strive for perfection, there will be rare errors or ommisions in different printings. These errors are corrected in subsequent printings as they are found. The contents of this guide, therefore, reflect the contents of the textbooks as they were intended to be printed, which may differ very slightly from what appears in a particular printing of the textbook.

Primary Language Lessons by Emma Serl, which this volume is meant to accompany, has been assigned a reading level of 490L. More information concerning this reading level assessment may be obtained by visiting www.lexile.com.

© Copyright August 2008
Lost Classics Book Company

ISBN 978-1-890623-33-3

Designed to Accompany
Primary Language Lessons by Emma Serl
ISBN 978-0-9652735-1-0

Contents

Objectives

The activities in this edition will meet the following objectives:

1. The student will identify words and construct meaning from text and illustrations, phonics and context clues.
2. The student will determine the main idea through illustrations.
3. The student will recognize basic patterns and functions of language.
4. The student will understand that word choice can shape ideas, feelings, and actions.
5. The student will use and identify repetition, rhyme, and rhythm in oral and written text.
6. The student will use text and previous readings to make predictions.
7. The student will use a simple outline.
8. The student will use knowledge of developmental-level vocabulary in reading.
9. The student will increase comprehension by retelling and discussion.
10. The student will recognize the beginning, middle, and end in passages.
11. The student will write questions and observations about familiar topics, stories, or new experiences.
12. The student will know the basic characteristics of fables, stories, and myths.
13. The student will use simple reference materials to obtain information.
14. The student will listen for a variety of purposes, including curiosity, pleasure, and directions. Students will also listen to perform tasks, solve problems, and follow rules.
15. The student will retell details of information including sequencing of information.
16. The student will produce final documents that have been edited for correct spelling, punctuation, capitalization, and sentence structure.
17. The student will use knowledge and experience to tell about experiences or to write for familiar occasions, audiences, and purposes.
18. The student will follow simple sets of instructions for simple tasks using logical sequencing of steps.
19. The student will use different forms of words, including contractions, possessive nouns, and present, past, and future tenses.
20. The student will determine how to draw conclusions from texts.
21. The student will understand sentence varieties, paragraph writing, and punctuation.

Lesson 1
A Picture Lesson—
Piper and Nutcrackers

Teacher Notes

Have students answer the questions orally or in writing.

1. What do you see in the picture?
2. Where are the squirrels?
3. What are they doing?
4. What season of the year is it?
5. What is the bird doing?
6. Tell about some squirrels you have seen.
7. Where do they live?
8. How did they prepare for the winter?
   Answers will vary to the questions above.
9. What is the name of the picture?
   The name of the picture is Piper and Nutcrackers.
10. What is the name of the artist who painted the picture from which this was copied?
    The name of the artist is Landseer.

Artist

The painting was done by English artist Sir Henry Landseer (1802–1873). He studied at the Royal Academy School in London, and is most famous for his animal paintings.

Subject

Squirrels are small day-active animals that have thick fur and bushy tails. They are often black, gray, or brown in color on their backs and a light color on their bellies. Squirrels are very agile and can leap from branch to branch easily. When they descend from a high place they always go down head first. Much of their time is spent on the ground looking for food. They like to eat fruit, nuts, and insects. They often store food for the winter in holes in the ground even though they do not hibernate. About 40 species of squirrels can be found in North and South America and throughout Europe.

Activities

1. Have students draw their own picture of a squirrel.
2. Have students color the picture of the squirrel on the next page.
3. Have students write or tell their own story about the squirrel they draw or color.
4. Have students read an encyclopedia article about squirrels and give a short report.

Lesson 2

Teacher Notes

Depending on students' ability, have them write in cursive. Worksheets are provided at the back of this book, page 118.

Lesson 3

Is—Are

Teacher Notes

Explain to students that the verb *is* is used with a singular subject, and *are* is used with a plural subject.

1. Two squirrels <u>are</u> in the tree.
2. A little bird <u>is</u> singing to them.
3. There <u>are</u> green leaves around them.
4. The blue sky <u>is</u> above them.
5. Nuts <u>are</u> ripe and the squirrels <u>are</u> happy.

Additional Exercises

1. The bird <u>is</u> blue.
2. Nuts <u>are</u> falling from the tree.
3. The little boy <u>is</u> watching the birds.
4. <u>Are</u> the squirrels saving nuts for the winter?
5. <u>Is</u> the bird stealing a nut?
6. The squirrels <u>are</u> on the branch.
7. The branch <u>is</u> going to crack.
8. There <u>are</u> too many nuts in the hole.
9. The little girl <u>is</u> happy to see the squirrels.
10. Spring <u>is</u> on its way.

Extended Activity

Have students write their own sentences using *is* and *are*. Students can write sentences using the following subjects: a little girl, a little boy, children, squirrels, birds.

Lesson 4
Selection to be Memorized—"If I Knew"

Extended Activities
1. Have students make a collage of different facial expressions. Have students label the expressions with appropriate adjectives.
2. Have students draw a picture of the first or second stanza of the poem.
3. Have students bring in a picture of themselves and share the occasion on which the picture was taken.
4. Using a digital camera, take pictures of your students making different expressions. Have students label the expressions. Post the pictures in your room.

Lesson 5
Observation Lesson—"Frost"

Teacher Notes
This lesson may not be appropriate for all students because of geographical location. You may use the Alternate Observation Lesson on rain if your students are unfamiliar with frost.

When does frost come?
Frost is ice that is formed when water vapor touches a surface that is at or below 32 degrees Fahrenheit. Therefore, frost comes when the weather outside begins to cool–fall and winter.
What does frost do to plants?
Frost can kill plants.
What plants are killed first by frost?
Delicate plants such as flowers and fruits are killed first.
Which plants last the longest in the fall?
Cold-resistant plants live longer in the fall.
What plants and trees cannot grow where you live, on account of the frost?
Answers will vary depending on geographical location.
What does the frost do to nut burs?
The frost can damage the burs, thus ruining the seed for future sprouting.
What effect does it have upon the air?
The air will be very cool when it frosts.

Alternate Observation Lesson
"Rain"
Where does rain come from?
Rain comes from the clouds in the sky.

What does rain do for plants?

Rain provides moisture for plants so they can grow.

What can happen if it rains too much?

If it rains too much, it can flood and can kill plants if they get too much water.

What can happen if it rains too little?

If it rains too little, plants can die. When it doesn't rain for a long time it is called a drought.

What kinds of plants need little water?

Plants such as cacti need little water.

What kinds of plants need many inches of rain?

Tropical plants such as palm trees need many inches of rain.

Extended Activities

1. Have students use the Internet and find out information on the observation lesson topics to answer the questions.
2. Students may draw a picture of rain or frost.
3. Students may research the rain cycle and draw a diagram of it.
4. Have students keep records of how much it rains in a week. Then have students write a paragraph explaining their findings.

LESSON 6
For Dictation

Teacher Notes

Writing and dictation worksheets are provided at the back of this book, page 118.

LESSON 7
Selection to be Memorized—"A Secret"

Teacher Notes

It may be helpful to use the memorization rubric at the back of this book, page 108.

With what kind of letter is the word *I* always written?

I is always written with a capital letter.

LESSON 8

Copy these sentences and fill in the blanks by referring to Lesson 7, page 5 of the textbook.

Teacher Notes
Writing and dictation worksheets are provided at the back of this book, page 118.

Answers
The robin and I and the sweet cherry tree have a secret.
The bird told the tree.
The tree told me.
Nobody knows it but just us three.
The robin knows the secret best.

LESSON 9
Dictation—"The Clouds"

Teacher Notes
Writing and dictation worksheets are provided at the back of this book, page 118.

LESSON 10
Presentation—Oral—"The Dog in the Manger"

Teacher Notes
The oral presentation rubric at the back of this book may be helpful, page 109.

LESSON 11
A Picture Lesson—
Wide Awake

The student may answer this lesson's questions in writing or out loud.

Below are suggested answers.
What do you see in the picture?
Three kittens are in the picture.
Where are the kittens?

The kittens are sitting in an old basket with a blanket, and hay around them.

If you had three kittens like these, what would you name them?

Answers will vary.

What is the name of this picture?

The name of this picture is Wide Awake.

What is the artist's name?

The artist's name is Adam.

Tell a story about kittens.

*Answers will vary. You might choose to read a story about kittens—*The Three Little Kittens *by Anna Alter,* The Cat in the Hat *by Dr. Suess, and* Prodigal Cat *by Janette Oke.*

Draw the kitten on the previous page.

Lesson 12
Observation Lesson

Read each question silently, and give the answer as a complete statement.

Suggested Answers

With what is a cat covered?

A cat is covered with fur.

Of what use is the fur?

The fur is used for protection and to provide warmth.

When is the fur the thickest?

The fur is the thickest in the winter to keep the cat warm.

When does a cat shed its fur?

The cat sheds its fur in the summer.

What does a cat eat?

An outdoor cat will eat rodents like rats or mice. An indoor or domesticated cat will eat processed cat food that its owner purchases from the store. Cats also like milk.

Of what use is a cat about a house or barn?

A cat is useful to keep out rodents.

Of what use are the soft cushions or pads on a cat's feet?

The soft cushions on a cat's feet are good for the silent stalking of prey.

Of what use are the claws?

The claws are good for hunting and self-defense.

How many claws has a cat on each forefoot? How many on each hind foot? Why does a cat need more claws on her forefeet than on her hind ones? Where are the claws when not in use? How does Puss keep them sharp?

A cat has five claws on each forefoot and four claws on each hindfoot. A cat needs more claws on her forefeet because they help her catch prey. When the claws are not in use, a cat keeps them retracted in the paw. It keeps them sharp by scraping them against a hard object.

What is the shape of the center of a cat's eye when she has been in the dark? How does it look when she has been in a strong light?

A cat's eye will look big and round when in the dark. The dilated pupils allow light in. When the cat is in strong light the pupils grow small, shaped like a vertical slit, to block out light.

What kind of teeth has a cat?

A cat has sharp teeth to help it capture and eat its prey.

Tell something about a cat's tongue.

A cat has a tongue with sharp spines on it. They help the cat when she eats and grooms herself.

Of what use are a cat's whiskers?

A cat's whiskers help her with navigation and sensation.

How does a cat carry her little ones? How does she keep them clean?

A cat carries her little ones by lifting the kittens by the back of their necks, and keeps the kittens clean by licking their fur.

Is it easy to teach a cat tricks?

No, it is not easy to teach a cat tricks.

Lesson 13

Composition

Write answers to the first six questions about the cat in Lesson 12, page 8 in the textbook.

In Lesson 3, page 2, you learned about *is* and *are*. In the answers you wrote, underline the word *is* and circle the word *are*.

Lesson 14

Conversation Lesson—"The Care of Pets"

Suggested Answers

If you had a pony, how would you take care of him?

One could take care of a pony by grooming him regularly. Brushing his mane and cleaning his hooves are part of grooming a pony.

What would you give him to eat?

One might give a pony cereals, carrots, or apples.

What does a pony need besides food?

A pony needs good care and exercise.

Tell some things that should not be done to a pony.

One should not walk behind a pony without letting him know you are there. He may kick you. Also, ponies should never be mistreated.

What could the pony do for you?

A pony could carry you places or carry items. A pony can also pull things such as wagons. A pony makes a good companion.

How would you take care of a canary bird?

To take care of a canary bird, one must feed it, house it in a clean cage, and give it a shallow dish for a bath.

What could a canary bird do in return for your care?

A canary bird can sing for you.

What care does a dog require?

A dog requires that you feed it and give it exercise. Dogs need baths to keep them clean and to make sure that they don't have fleas or ticks.

What could a dog do for you?

A dog can be your friend. It can fetch items such as a newspaper or slippers for you.

Do you know any story about a dog's helping someone?

Some stories about dogs helping someone are Lassie, *by Eric Knight, and Rin Tin Tin adventure stories.*

What tricks can you teach a dog?

You can teach a dog to sit, play dead, and fetch.

What other animals are good pets?

Answers will vary.

Tell how to take care of them.

Answers will vary.

How many questions are there in this lesson?

Fifteen questions are in this lesson.

What mark of punctuation is placed after each question?

A question mark is placed at the end of each question.

Extended Activities:

1. Students may draw pictures of the animals discussed in Lesson 14.
2. Students may use the Internet to research one or more of the animals in Lesson 14.
3. Have the students select someone who owns an animal that interests them. Have students develop a list of questions to use to interview a pet owner. Once the questions are written, have the students interview the person and record the answers.
4. For a field trip, visit a zoo. Allow students to ask questions about an animal that interests them. Have students then write a paragraph on what they learned. Use the composition rubric provided in the back of this book, page 110, to score the paragraph.

Lesson 15

For Copying and Dictation—*To-Too-Two*

To, too, and *two* are homophones. Homophones are words that sound the same, but are spelled differently and have different meanings. *To* is a preposition and is also part of the infinitive form of a verb. *Too* is an adverb that means also or too much. *Two* is the number *2.*

1. *Two* pints make one quart.
2. This work is not *too* hard for me.
3. Mother sent me *to* the store.
4. She told me *to* buy some meat, and some eggs, *too*.
5. *Two* boys went *to* the river.

Lesson 16

Copy the sentences, filling in the blanks with to, too, or two.

1. *Two* boys were flying a kite.
2. It is not *too* cold to play in the yard.
3. *Two* squirrels live in the old oak tree.
4. The children like *to* watch them.
5. Do not go *too* close *to* the edge of the pond.
6. Mary went *to* church, and her sister went, *too*.
7. The doll cost *two* dollars. I think it cost *too* much.
8. It takes *two* *to* make a quarrel.
9. Do not sing *too* loud.
10. *Two* and *two* are four.
11. The sun gives light *to* the moon.
12. I saw *two* bright stars in the sky.

Extended Activity
Write sentences using the words you just learned. Writing and dictation worksheets are provided in the back of this book, page 118.

Lesson 17
Reproduction—Oral— "The Lion and the Fox"

After students read and/or write the story, have them answer the following questions.

1. Why did the lion pretend to be sick?
   The lion pretended to be sick because he was too old and weak to go out and hunt for food.
2. Some animals were tricked when they came to help the lion. What do their actions tell you about them?

The animals who were tricked were willing to help the lion. Their actions show that they are kind and may be somewhat naive.

3. **Who do you think was more clever, the lion, or the fox?**

    Answers will vary.

4. **What characteristics are often attributed to the lion? To the fox? Do the lion and the fox fit these descriptions?**

    A characteristic often attributed to the lion is courage and is called "the king of the beasts." Foxes are thought to be cunning and sly. The lion does not seem to fit this characteristic because he is old and sick, whereas the fox does fit the description. The fox was wise enough to see past the lion's deception.

5. **What do you think happened at the end of the story when the fox told the lion he noticed footprints going into the den, but none coming out? Create an ending to the story.**

    Answers will vary.

Lesson 18
Selection to be Memorized—"Lady Moon"

Refer to memorization rubric at the back of this book for evaluation, page 108.

Lesson 19
Was—Were

Was is a singular verb. The verb *were* is used with a plural subject or as a singular past tense when used with the pronoun *you*. Students are to read the four sentences and then answer the questions that follow.

How many boys are mentioned in the first sentence?

   One

Is *was* or *were* used in that sentence?

   Was

How many boys are mentioned in the second sentence?

   Two

Is *was* or *were* used in that sentence?

   Were

In which sentence is *you* used?

   Sentence #3

Is *was* or *were* used with *you*?

   Were

In which sentence are a number of children mentioned?

   Sentence #4

Is *was* or *were* used in that sentence?

   Were

Copy these sentences, filling in the blanks with *was* or *were*.

1. The day _was_ very warm.
2. The boys _were_ swimming in the pond.
3. _Were_ they having a good time?
4. You _were_ not at school yesterday.
5. _Were_ you sick?
6. Two dogs _were_ playing in the road.
7. One dog _was_ run over by a wagon.
8. Its foot _was_ hurt.
9. The children _were_ sorry for the poor dog.

Lesson 20

Copy the sentences in Lesson 3, filling the blanks with *was* or *were*. Use *was* in speaking of one; use *were* in speaking of one or more, or with the word *you*.

1. Two squirrels _were_ in the tree.
2. A little bird _was_ singing to them.
3. There _were (leaves is the subject)_ green leaves around them.
4. The blue sky _was_ above them.
5. Nuts _were_ ripe and the squirrels _were_ happy.

Extended Activity

The following is a review quiz for lessons 1-20.
Select the correct word for each sentence.

1. It (_was_, were) a warm spring.
2. Tom and Sam (is, _are_) going swimming.
3. Tom (_was_, were) a very good swimmer.
4. Tom and Sam (is, _are_) on the swim team at school.
5. Sam (_is_, are) the fastest swimmer on the team.
6. Tom (_was_, were) the fastest until he hurt his arm.
7. (_Is_, Are) he going to get better?

Lesson 21
For Dictation and Oral Reproduction—"Wheat"

Refer to oral reading rubric at the back of this book for evaluation, page 111.

Lesson 22

Observation Lesson—Trees

Students may need to use the Internet or the encyclopedia to find the answers to these questions. Answers may depend on the students' geographical location.

Name three kinds of shade trees.
Oak, Maple, Weeping Willow, etc. are shade trees. Any tree with large leaves and big branches can be considered a shade tree.

Name eight kinds of fruit trees.
Banana, pear, peach, lemon, lime, apple, cherry, orange, grapefruit, etc. are kinds of fruit trees.

Name five kinds of nut trees.
The chestnut, almond, pecan, walnut, and hickory are five kinds of nut trees.

Name five kinds of trees whose wood is used for lumber.
Pine, cherry, maple, oak, and walnut are trees used for lumber.

Name some kinds of trees that grow only in warm countries.
Citrus trees grow in warm countries. Other trees that grow in warm countries are called tropical trees. These include the palm tree (coconut, for example), mahogany, teak, rosewood, and others.

Name some kinds of trees that remain green all winter.
Trees that remain green all winter are usually called evergreen trees. These would include the pine, spruce and fir tree.

Draw a picture containing three trees.

Extended Activities

1. Have students research different trees and make a poster with a picture and description of each of them.
2. Students may make a two-column chart of the trees that live in warm climates and trees that live in cold climates.
3. Have students write a poem or description of a tree.

Lesson 23

A Picture Lesson—*Saved*

Tell what you see in the picture.
The picture shows a dog by an ocean or lake with a girl lying on its front two legs. The sky looks gray and cloudy.

How do you suppose the child happened to fall into the water?
Answers will vary. Possibly the girl tripped or fell

into the water by mistake while trying to look at something in the water, or perhaps she was rescued from a sinking ship.

Where was the dog?

Answers will vary. More than likely, the dog was with the girl when she went by the water.

What did he do?

It seems that the dog saved the girl.

What is the name of this picture?

The name of this picture is Saved.

What is the name of the artist?

The name of the artist is Landseer.

Write a story about this picture. Worksheets are provided at the back of this book, page 118.

Lesson 24

A—An

A comes before a word beginning with a consonant, and *an* comes before a word beginning with a vowel. *A*, *an*, and *the* are types of adjectives called *articles*. They introduce nouns.

Copy
1. Lucy found an egg in a nest in the barn.
2. An eagle builds its nest in the mountains.
3. Hiawatha was an Indian boy.
4. Frank paid two cents for an apple.
5. Have you seen the nest of an oriole?
6. I saw an ugly dog yesterday.

Do the words that follow *an* begin with vowels or consonants?

Vowel. Vowel letters are A, E, I, O, U and sometimes Y

Extended Activity

Have students underline the *a* or *an* in the sentences and circle the letter of the word that follows.

Lesson 25

Copy these sentences, filling in the blanks with *a* or *an*.

1. *An* owl sat on *a* branch of *a* tree.
2. Tom bought *an* orange and *a* banana.
3. *An* army of men marched up the hill.
4. *An* old man was playing on *a* harp.
5. *An* ape is something like *a* monkey.
6. The girl wanted *an* ice cream soda.
7. Henry saw *an* elephant and *a* tiger.

Lesson 26
Days of the Week

Sunday	Thursday
Monday	Friday
Tuesday	Saturday
Wednesday	

With what kind of letter does the name of each day begin?
Each day begins with a capital letter.

Copy these sentences, filling the blanks:
1. There are *seven* days in the week.
2. The first day of the week is *Sunday*.
3. We go to school on *Monday*, *Tuesday*, *Wednesday*, *Thursday*, and *Friday*.
4. We play on *Saturday*.
5. We go to church on *Sunday*.

Do not allow students to abbreviate the days. Additionally, based on the child's religious affiliation, #2 may be Sunday and #5 may be Saturday.

Lesson 27
Composition—Oral or Written

When will you have your next vacation?
What do you expect to do then?

Use the oral presentation or essay rubric at the back of this book to score this lesson, pages 109 or 113.

Activities
1. Students mayn write a report based on a past or future vacation. Use the essay rubric at the back of this book to evaluate the essay.
2. Have students put together a "show and tell" of a past vacation. Have them share with you or the class.
3. Have students write, research, or orally describe a vacation they would like to have.
4. Have students locate on a map where their vacation occurred.

Lesson 28
Selection to be Memorized—"The Swing"

How many pictures can you find in this poem?
There are three pictures in this poem:
1. a child swinging against a blue sky,
2. a picture of the countryside with rivers, trees and cattle, and
3. a green garden and a brown roof.

Draw one of them.
With what kind of letter does the first word of every line of poetry begin?
Each line begins with a capital letter.

Use the memorization rubric at the back of this book to evaluate this lesson, page 108.

Lesson 29
When?

Copy these sentences, filling in the blanks with words that answer the question *When?*

Suggested Answers
1. The violets bloom <u>*in the spring*</u>.

2. *In the morning* **I eat breakfast.**
3. **We have dinner** *in the evening*.
4. *On Sundays* **we go to church.**
5. **I like to go to the woods** *in the afternoon*.
6. **The farmer plants corn** *in the summer*.
7. **The stars shine** *at night*.
8. *In the evening* **the sun is in the west.**
9. **The owl sleeps** *at night*.

Lesson 30
Composition

What did you do last Saturday morning?
What did you do in the afternoon?
Write your answers in this form:

> *Last Saturday morning I _____.*
> *In the afternoon I _____.*

Use the essay rubric at the back of this book, page 113, to evaluate this composition. Pay particular attention to the proper capitalization of the days of the week.

Lesson 31
Oral and Written— "The Rabbit"

Suggested Answers
With what is a rabbit covered?
> *A rabbit is covered with fur.*

Describe a rabbit's ears.
> *Its ears are long and floppy.*

What kind of teeth has a rabbit?
> *A rabbit has incisors which are small, delicate teeth used for gnawing.*

Name two other animals that have teeth like a rabbit's.
> *Two other animals who have teeth like a rabbit's are the mouse and gerbil.*

3. Can you think of any other plan the mice could have created to get rid of the cat?
4. Draw a picture of the kind of bell you think the mice were going to put on the cat.

Lesson 36
Where?

Copy these sentences, filling the blanks with words that answer the question *Where?*

Answers for each sentence will vary. However, every answer should begin with a preposition—in, by, on, down. For example: 1. <u>In the yard</u> stood a large pine tree.

1. _____ stood a large pine tree.
2. _____ were some little boys playing marbles.
3. _____ was a little bird's nest.
4. _____ grew blue violets and yellow buttercups.
5. _____ was a big red automobile that had broken down.
6. _____ was a bush covered with beautiful roses.
7. _____ were two busy squirrels.
8. _____ came the fire engine.
9. _____ stood the wigwam of Nokomis.
10. _____ were the busy bees.
11. _____ lived a mother rabbit and her little ones.
12. _____ were three little kittens.

Lesson 37
Oral and Written—*Has—Have*

Copy these sentences:
1. I have a new book.
2. We have new books.
3. Tom has a little sister.
4. You have the wrong answer.
5. They have their fishing rods.
6. The rabbit has long ears.

Extended Activities
1. Have students underline the word have or has in each sentence.
2. Have students identify the subject of each sentence as being singular or plural. What do the verbs have in common with the verbs *was* and *were* from Lesson 19, page 14 in the textbook?

Fill in these blanks with has or have:
1. *Have* you seen the river?
2. Nellie *has* a canary bird.
3. Harry and Nellie *have* roller skates.
4. They *have* ice skates, too.
5. The oriole *has* a nest in that tree.
6. I *have* a drawing pencil.
7. Rover *has* a new collar.
8. *Have* you seen it?
9. It *has* his name on it.
10. The horse *has* gone.

Lesson 38
A Picture Lesson—
The Escaped Cow

Tell what you see in the picture.

The picture is of a boy chasing a cow in a field.

What time of day do you think it is? What makes you think so?

The time of day seems to be in the morning or afternoon because the sky is light and the boy is wearing a hat to keep the sun off his face.

What is the boy doing?

The boy is herding a cow back to the herd, using a stick to direct it.

What kind of shoes has he?

He is wearing wooden clogs.

In what country do they wear such shoes?

People who live in Holland wear these kinds of shoes.

What is the woman doing?

The woman is milking a cow.

What is the name of the picture?

The name of the picture is The Escaped Cow.

What is the artist's name?

The artist's name is Dupré.

Lesson 39
Observation Lesson—The Cow

What animal gives us milk?

The cow gives us milk.

What forms on top of the milk after it has stood awhile?

Cream forms on top of the milk after it has stood awhile.

Name some things that are made from milk.

Cheese, butter, yogurt, and cream are products made from milk.

Tell how butter is made.

Butter is made by putting the cream into a churn. The churn mixes the cream making the butterfat stick together. Once this has been done, and there is a significant amount of butterfat, the remaining buttermilk is drained. Sometimes salt is added to preserve the butter.

What is the flesh of the cow called?

The flesh of a cow is called beef.

What use is made of the cow's hide?

Leather products are made from the hide.

What things are made from her horns?

Accessories such as belt buckles, ornaments for a room, shoe horns and jewelry are made from the horns of a cow.

What is made from her hoofs?

Glue and gelatin are made from the hoofs of a cow.

What use is made of the hair on the cow?

The hair of the cow can be used for coverings such as coats or furniture.

Activities

1. Students may need to do some basic research in an encyclopedia or Internet to answer the questions for this lesson.
2. Have the students make their own butter. Put a small amount of cream into a jar (a baby food jar works best.) Shake the jar until butter begins to form. Shaking the jar will take some time. Once a clump of butter has formed in the jar, empty out the remaining milk that has not hardened.
3. Have students discuss the benefits of milk.

Lesson 40
Composition—Description

Answers will vary for this lesson.

Lesson 41
Composition

Write sentences telling something about each:
dog
rabbit
bluejay
horse
squirrel
oriole
owl
robin
eagle

Extended Activities

1. Have students identify which of the animals in the list are types of birds. Have students name types of dogs and horses.
2. Instead of students writing a sentence about each animal, have them write or tell a story with these animals.
3. Create puppets of each of the animals made of small brown bags. Have the students create dialogue and/or a story using the puppets.

Lesson 42
The Seasons and Months of the Year

The seasons are spring, summer, autumn, and winter.
The months are:

January	July
February	August
March	September
April	October
May	November
June	December

With what kind of letter does the name of each month begin? Each season?

Each month begins with a capital letter. Each season begins with a lower case letter, unless it is the first word in a sentence.

For Dictation

Writing and dictation worksheets are provided in the back of this book, page 118.

Extended Activities

1. Have students make a chart for the seasons and months.
2. Have students take a piece of paper and divide it into four parts. Draw a picture representing each of the four seasons in each corner.

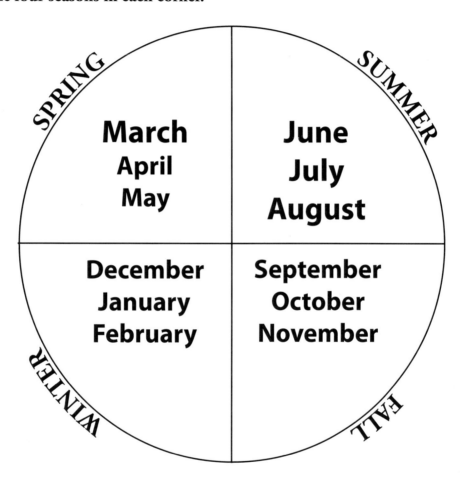

Lesson 43

What Month?

Copy these sentences, filling in the blanks with words that answer the question *What Month?*

1. Christmas comes in *December*.
2. Washington's birthday is in *February*.
3. School begins in *answers will vary*.
4. Thanksgiving is in *November*.

5. New Year's is the first day of _January_.
6. _June_ is called the "month of roses."
7. Easter usually comes in _March or April_.
8. Decoration Day is in _May (Decoration Day is now called Memorial Day)_.
9. _February (28 days, except in leap year, then there are 29)_ is the shortest month.
10. My birthday is in _answers will vary_.

Extended Activities

1. Have students identify the month for the following American holidays: January—Martin Luther King Day; February—Valentine's Day, Presidents' Day; March—St. Patrick's Day; May—Pearl Harbor Remembrance Day, Mother's Day; June—Father's Day; July—Independence Day; October—Columbus Day, Halloween; November—Election Day, Veteran's Day.
2. Have students memorize the saying: "Thirty days has September, April, June, and November; All the rest have thirty-one except for February, which has twenty-eight."
3. Have students complete the calendar for the current month. A blank calendar can be found at the back of this book, page 115.

Lesson 44
What Season?

Copy the sentences, filling the blanks with words that answer the question, _What season?_

1. In _winter_ the days are short and the nights are long.
2. In _summer_ the days are long and the nights are short.
3. The farmer sows his corn in the _spring_.
4. In the _autumn_ squirrels gather nuts.
5. We skate and make snowballs in _winter_.
6. The birds go South in the _winter_; in the _spring_ they come back to us.

Lesson 45
See—Saw—Seen

To show the time of action or an expressed idea, verbs may change form. The time indicated by the change of form is called _tense_. See is present tense, and saw is past tense. The helping verbs _has_ or _have_ added to _seen_ is the present perfect tense. The helping verb _had_ added to _seen_ is the past perfect tense.

1. From my window I can see the river.
2. I saw a boat on the river yesterday.
3. I have seen larger boats on the lake.
4. My brother has seen the ocean.
5. I thought that you had seen the ocean.

What word is used before seen in the third sentence on page 33?
Have is the word used before seen in the third sentence.
What word is used before seen in the fourth sentence?
Has is the word used before seen in the fourth sentence.
What word is used before seen in the fifth sentence?
Had is the word used before seen in the fifth sentence.

Copy these sentences, filling in the blanks with *see, saw,* or *seen.*
1. I can <u>see</u> the blue sky and the fleecy white clouds.
2. I <u>saw</u> a rainbow last summer.
3. I have <u>seen</u> heavy black clouds in the west.
4. Last fall we <u>saw</u> red and yellow leaves on the maple trees.
5. In the spring we shall <u>see</u> wild flowers in the woods.
6. Have you <u>seen</u> apple trees in blossom?
7. I <u>saw</u> a little brook in the woods.
8. I have <u>seen</u> the bees gathering honey.
9. Last summer we <u>saw</u> a robin's nest in the elm tree.
10. Did you <u>see</u> the humming bird among the lilies?

Lesson 46
Selection to be Memorized— "The Brown Thrush"

Refer to the memorization rubric, page 108.
After reading the poem, answer the following questions.

Where is the brown thrush?
A "merry brown thrush (is) sitting up in the tree."
What is he doing?
The brown thrush is "singing to me."
Why is he so happy?
The brown thrush is happy because there are eggs in the nest.
Where is his nest?

The nest is "in the juniper tree."

How many eggs are there in the nest?

"Five eggs" are in the nest.

Copy what the thrush says in the last stanza.

In the last stanza the thrush says, "Oh, the world's running over with joy! But long it won't be, Don't you know? Don't you see? Unless we are as good as can be."

Extended Activities

1. **Stanzas are paragraphs of a poem. How many stanzas are there in this poem?**

    There are three stanzas in this poem.

2. **Discuss what could happen to the eggs if a child was to meddle with them.**

Lesson 47
Composition

Reread the story, "The Dog in the Manger," on page 6; then close your book and write it from memory.

A dog lay in a manger in which was placed hay for the oxen.
At noon the oxen came to eat their dinner.
The dog growled and snapped at them, and would not let them have even a mouthful.
"You selfish fellow," said an ox, "you cannot eat the hay. Why won't you let us have it?"

Extended Activities

1. **Have students write an ending to this story.**
2. **Discuss reasons why the dog would not let the oxen eat.**

Lesson 48
Composition

Copy these sentences and fill in the blanks with the words that answer the question, *How?*

Specific answers will vary. Below are suggestions.

1. **The children did their work _quietly_.**
2. **The dog barked _loudly_.**

3. Nellie sews _neatly_.
4. The wind blew _wildly_.
5. The fire horses ran _quickly_.
6. Trees grow _slowly_.
7. The cat purrs _softly_.
8. The lion roared _loudly_.
9. The bird sings _beautifully_.
10. The engineer blew the whistle _loudly_.
11. The man spoke _nicely_ to the child.
12. The mother cat carried her kittens _gently_ to another home.

Answers will be adverbs. An adverb is a part of speech that describes a verb, an adjective, or another adverb. Most adverbs end in –_ly_.

Lesson 49
Letter Writing

Copy the letter from Frank to George.

Draw the envelope and copy the address upon it.

What mark of punctuation is placed after _Ave._?
The period indicates that Ave. stands for the word Avenue.

Where should the stamp be placed on an envelope?
A stamp ought to be placed in the top right hand corner of the envelope.

Master is the title given to an unmarried young man. _Mr._ is a title given to an older man. _Miss_ is a title given to a single young woman, _Mrs._ is the title for a married woman and _Ms._ is a title given to an older single woman. Students will be either _Master_ or _Miss_.

Extended Activities
Have the students address a second envelope to a friend or relative. The return address goes in the top left hand corner of an envelope.

Envelope outlines can be found at the back of this book, page 116.

Atlanta, Ga.
Jan. 25, 1910
Dear George,
    I hear that you have some rabbits to sell. I want to buy two, if they do not cost too much.
    Have you any white ones? How much are they? When may I come to see them?
    Let me hear from you soon.
        Your friend,
        Frank Martin.

Master George Andrews
2116 Maple Ave.
Atlanta
Georgia

Lesson 50
Letter Writing

Write George's answer to Frank.
Draw the envelope and direct it to:

Master Frank Martin
1518 South Tenth Street
Atlanta, GA 30341

Envelope outlines can be found at the back of this book, page 116.

Lesson 51
Directing Envelopes

Draw five envelopes and direct them as follows:
  1. To Mr. Ralph Barton, 1407 Grand Ave., Portland, Oregon 97232
  2. To Mrs. S.W. Gray, 320 Main St., Dallas Texas 75202
  3. To your teacher
  4. To yourself
  5. To a friend who lives in a city in some other state than your own.

Envelope outlines can be found at the back of this book, page 116.

Mr. Ralph Barton 1407 Grand Ave. Portland, Oregon 97232

Mrs. S. W. Gray 320 Main Street Dallas, Texas 75202

Lesson 52
Conversation Lesson— "Preparation for Winter"

How do the plants and trees get ready for winter?
  Plants and trees get ready for winter by losing their leaves.

What preparation does the squirrel make?

The squirrel collects and stores food so that he can eat during the winter months.

Name another animal that stores away food.

Other animals that store food are mice and beavers.

Where do toads and frogs spend the winter?

Toads and frogs spend the winter hibernating or burying themselves in mud. These animals are cold-blooded and their bodies slow down as it gets cold. Some have been known to survive totally frozen.

What becomes of snakes?

Snakes hibernate in the winter.

What birds go South?

Some birds that go South for the winter are ducks, geese, robins, and swans.

What change is there in the covering of those that remain?

Birds that remain grow more feathers to keep them warm.

How do bears spend the winter?

Bears spend the winter hibernating like many other animals. Hibernation is a deep sleep.

What insects prepare food for the winter?

Insects that prepare food for the winter are bees and spiders.

What becomes of the other insects?

Other insects die in the winter. They will often lay eggs that will hatch when the weather warms.

What does the caterpillar do?

A caterpillar will build a cocoon and sleep during the winter.

What difference is there in the coats of horses, dogs and other animals.

The coats of animals such as horses and dogs will become thick to keep the animal warm.

Lesson 53
A Picture Lesson—
Shoeing the Horse

What is a man who shoes horses called?

A man who shoes horses is called a ferrier.

What other work does he do?

He also has limited knowledge in veterinary medicine. A ferrier specializes in the lower limbs of a horse. He also is similar to a blacksmith in that he molds and makes tools.

What tools does he use?

The forge, hammer, and anvil are some of the tools used by a ferrier.

Tell what you see in the picture.

The picture shows a ferrier putting a horseshoe on

the hind foot of a horse. There are also a dog and donkey in the picture.

Write a story about the picture, telling about the horse's master, where the shoe was lost, why the donkey is in the shop, what the dog's name is, and why he came with the horse. Tell other things the picture suggests.

Use the story rubric at the back of this book, page 112, to evaluate this composition. Make sure in evaluating that the student has addressed all five questions above.

Another picture by Landseer is *Saved* on page 17 and *Piper and Nutcrackers* on page xii.

Lessons 54 and 55
For Dictation

Erito is a little Eskimo boy. His home is in Greenland.
  It is very cold there.
He lives in an igloo. His father made it of blocks of
  ice.
Erito's clothes are made of skins of animals. He looks
  like a little bear.
There are no horses where Erito lives. His father owns many dogs. These dogs are taught to pull
  heavy loads.
Erito has two big dogs. He hitches these to his sled, and they draw him over the ice and snow.
Many animals live near his home. There are big white bears and seals. There are reindeer, too.
  Erito hopes to be a hunter some day.

Lesson 56
Why?

Copy these sentences, filling the blanks with words that answer the question, *Why?*

Answers will vary. By answering the question why *after the word* because, *students are writing dependent clauses. A clause is a group of words with a subject and predicate that begins with a subordinating conjunction. The word* because *is a subordinating conjunction. A dependent clause cannot stand alone; it must be connected to an independent clause.*
  Example answer: James was late at school because he missed the bus.
  1. James was late at school because _____.
  2. Nellie did not know her lesson because _____.
  3. The squirrels had nuts to eat all winter because _____.
  4. Tom's garden did not grow because _____.
  5. The sun did not shine because _____.

6. I like to go to the woods in summer because _____.
7. Minnie did not go to the picnic because _____.
8. The boys like to play with Frank because _____.
9. They do not like to play with Arthur because _____.
10. The boy was praying because _____.

Lesson 57

Selection to be Memorized—"Dutch Lullaby"

Use the memorization rubric at the back of this book, page 108, to evaluate.

Extended Activities

After reading the poem, have students answer the following questions:
1. How many stanzas are in this poem?
    Four
2. What is the rhyme scheme of this poem?
    Rhyme scheme can be found by identifying the pattern of the end rhyme of each stanza. For example, the first stanza's rhyming words are:
    Night - A
    Shoe - B
    Light - A
    Dew - B
    Wish - C
    Three - D
    Fish - C
    Sea - D
    We - D
    Each word that rhymes gets the same letter of the alphabet. Therefore, the rhyme scheme of this stanza is ABABCDCDD.
3. In what did Wynken, Blynken, and Nod sail?
    A wooden shoe
4. What were the herring fish in stanza two?
    The stars
5. In stanza four, what are Wynken and Blynken? Who is Nod?
    Wynken and Blynken are "two little eyes" and Nod is "a little head."

Have students illustrate a picture based on this poem.

Lesson 58
The Comma

A horse can run and trot and gallop and walk.
A horse can run, trot, gallop, and walk.

How many times is *and* used in the first sentence?
> *The word* and *is used three times in the first sentence.*

How many times is *and* used in the second sentence?
> And *is used only once in the second sentence.*

Where are the commas used in the second sentence?
> *The commas are used to list the four things a horse can do.*

Do not use *and* more than once in any one sentence of the following:

Suggested answers below (pay particular attention to the comma placement. Note that it is not necessary to place a comma between the second item and the word and. This is an optional comma.)

1. **Write a sentence telling three things that a bird can do.**
    A bird can sing, fly, and soar.
2. **Write a sentence telling four things that a cat can do.**
    A cat can jump, climb, run, and meow.
3. **Write a sentence telling three things that a baby can do.**
    A baby can cry, crawl, and laugh.
4. **Write a sentence telling three things that a carpenter can do.**
    A carpenter can saw, hammer, and cut wood.

Lesson 59
Observation Lesson—Seeds

What seeds are scattered by the wind?
> *Flower seeds such as the dandelion and seeds of weeds are scattered by the wind. Some seeds like the cottonwood seed can blow many miles. Some seeds, like that of the maple, twirl like helicopters when blown by the wind.*

What seeds are scattered by clinging to the fur of animals and to the clothing of people?
> *These same seeds are carried by clinging to the fur of animals and to the clothing of people. When an animal or person walks through a field, these seeds will attach themselves to fur or clothing.*

What seeds are carried by birds?
> *Birds can pick up seeds and drop them when they eat the fruit around the seed. A cherry is an example of a fruit a bird eats then drops its seed.*

What seeds have shells?

The pumpkin seed and the sunflower seed are examples of seeds with shells.

What seeds grow in pods?

Peas and peanuts are types of seeds that grow in pods.

What seeds have husks around them?

Corn is a plant whose seeds have a husk around them.

What seeds have pulp around them?

Fruit seeds have pulp around them.

Extended Activities

1. Give the children a pea pod or a peanut pod and have them open it up. Let students describe orally or in writing what they observe.
2. Let students plant a seed then keep a journal of its growth.
3. Take students outside to see if they can gather any seeds from the ground. Let them share orally or in writing what they found.

Lesson 60
Reproduction—Oral and Written— "The Greedy Dog"

After reading have students answer the following questions:

1. Why did the dog drop his piece of meat?
2. Explain why this story is a good lesson for greedy people.
3. Draw a Venn Diagram listing greedy behavior and kind, benevolent behavior. An empty Venn Diagram can be found at the back of this book, page 117.

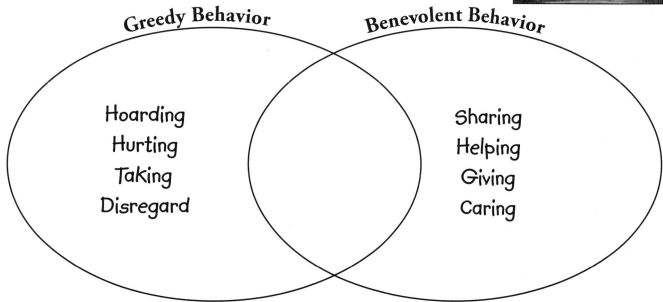

Greedy Behavior

Hoarding
Hurting
Taking
Disregard

Benevolent Behavior

Sharing
Helping
Giving
Caring

Lesson 61
Capitals

Copy
> **Chicago**
> **Texas**
> **Abraham Lincoln**
> **New York**
> **Kansas**
> **George Washington**

With what kind of letter does the name of a person or place begin?
> *A person or place begins with a capital letter.*

Below, answers will vary. Students can use an atlas, dictionary, or web site to find answers to #6-11. When evaluating students' answers, check for capitalization.
1. **Write your father's name.**
2. **Write the name of your teacher.**
3. **Write the names of three girls.**
4. **Write the names of three boys.**
5. **Write the name of the state in which you live.**
6. **Write the name of the governor of your state.**
7. **Write the name of the capital of your state.**
8. **Write the name of the largest city in your state.**
9. **Write the name of the President of the United States.**
10. **Write the name of the capital of the United States.**
11. **Write the name of the largest city in the United States.**

Lesson 62
Observation Lesson—Materials

Possible Answers
> *Chairs and tables are made of wood or metal.*
> *Railroad tracks are made of steel.*
> *Shoes are made of leather.*
> *Calico is made of clay. (Calico is a pattern on pottery.)*
> *Linen is made of cotton.*
> *Some buildings are made of brick, and some are made of steel or wood.*
> *Bricks are made of clay.*

Some money is made of paper, and some is made of silver or copper.
Needles are made of steel wire.
Paper is made of wood.
Warm clothes are made of wool.
Glass is made of sand or limestone.
Some candles are made of wax, and some are made of oil.
Horseshoes are made of metal.
Nails are made of metal.

Students can go to the web site askjeeves.com and type the question, "What is _____ made of?" to get an answer.

Lesson 63
Initials

Henry Wadsworth Longfellow
Henry W. Longfellow
H. W. Longfellow
H. W. L.

The first letter of a word is its initial letter.
What is the initial letter of Henry?
   H
Of Wadsworth?
   W
Of Longfellow?
   L
The first letters of a name are called initials.
What mark of punctuation follows an initial when used alone?
   A period.
With what kind of letter is an initial written?
   A capital.
Copy these names, using the initial instead of the middle name:
Ralph Waldo Emerson
   Ralph W. Emerson
John Greenleaf Whittier
   John G. Whittier
Edwin Henry Landseer
   Edwin H. Landseer
William Makepeace Thackeray
   William M. Thackeray

Copy these names using the initial instead of the first name:

Theodore Roosevelt

> *T. Roosevelt*

Charles Dickens

> *C. Dickens*

Walter Scott

> *W. Scott*

Daniel Webster

> *D. Webster*

Copy these names using the initials instead of the first and middle names:

Edgar Allan Poe

> *E. A. Poe*

Julia Ward Howe

> *J. W. Howe*

Henry Ward Beecher

> *H. W. Beecher*

Ulysses Simpson Grant

> *U. S. Grant*

Extended Activities

Have students create a monogram of their name. A monogram is a design made up of letters, usually the initials of a name. The middle letter is usually the last initial and is printed larger than the two letters that flank it. Students can use the sample font below to help them draw their monogram or if students have access to a word processor, allow them to create their monogram using the computer. Students should color it.

Edgar Allan Poe

EPA

A B C D E F G H I J K L M N O P Q R S T U V W X Y Z

Lesson 64
Selection to be Read and Studied— "The Journey"

After reading the selection, have students answer the following questions:

1. On what type of transportation is the speaker traveling?

The speaker is traveling on a train, stanza three.

2. **How many stanzas are there in the poem?**

There are 13 stanzas in the poem.

3. **Make a list of the rhyming words.**

Rhyming words: far-are, thick-pick, train-windowpane, still-hill, spires-wires, down-town, cup-up, burnt-weren't, roar-before, light-night, rise-eyes, door-roar, see- me.

4. **Who is the author? What are her initials?**

The author is Josephine Preston Peabody. Her initials are J. P. P.

5. **How does one punctuate the title of a poem? What is the title of this poem?**

The title of a poem goes in quotation marks. The title is "The Journey."

Answers below will vary. If students have not traveled by train, ask them in what they have traveled. If they traveled by car or plane, have students answer the questions from that perspective. Additionally, if students have not traveled by train, have them research trains. Is there a train station in your city? How have trains changed over the years? Besides transporting people, what other items do trains carry?

Did you ever journey on a train?

Where did you go?

What things did you see from the window?

Did you see anything that is spoken of in this poem?

How many pictures can you find?

Draw two of them.

Lesson 65

Observation Lesson—What Color?

Copy these sentences, filling the blanks with words that answer the question, *Of what color?*

1. **Grass is green.**
2. **Gold is yellow.**
3. **Salt is white.**
4. **The sky is blue.**
5. **Coal is black.**
6. **Bananas are yellow.**
7. **Wild roses are red or pink.**
8. **Cherries are red.**
9. **In autumn the maple leaves are red and yellow.**
10. **A watermelon is green on the outside and pink on the inside.**
11. **A woodpecker has a red head.**
12. **Daisies are white and yellow.**
13. **Some grapes are green, and some are purple.**

Extended Activity

1. Have students draw a rainbow and color it. The colors are red, orange, yellow, green, blue, indigo, and violet. A way to remember the colors is the mnemonic, ROY G. BIV.
2. Using a box of 64 crayons, have students identify the different shades of red, blue, and green. Have students scribble the color and then label it.
3. The names of the colors are primary sight words. Have students make flashcards with the name of the color written on them. Have students write the word using the color of the word.

Lesson 66
Letter Writing

Copy this letter:

> Detroit, Mich.
> May 10, 1911
>
> Dear Bessie,
> I found out that to-morrow is your birthday, and I am sending you a box of letter paper for a present. I hope you will have many happy birthdays.
> Your friend,
> Lillian Edwards.

Use the writing and dictation worksheet at the back of this book, page 118.

Teacher Note:
To-morrow is now written correctly as an unhyphenated word—tomorrow.

Lesson 67
Letter Writing

Write Bessie's answer to Lillian's letter, thanking her for the present and telling what other presents she received.

Draw an envelope and direct it. Lillian lives at 2632 Walnut St., Detroit, Michigan 33625

A blank envelope can be found at the back of this book.

```
┌─────────────────────────────────────────────────────┐
│ Return Address                                 Stamp │
│                                                       │
│                                                       │
│              Miss Lillian Edwards                     │
│              2632 Walnut St.                          │
│              Detroit, Michigan  33625                 │
│                                                       │
│                                                       │
└─────────────────────────────────────────────────────┘
```

Extended Activity

Have students write a letter to someone thanking them for a present or help that was given. Read *The Giving Tree*, by Shel Silverstein. Have students write a thank you letter to their mom and/or dad. Have students thank their parent(s) for the little things their parents have done for them.

Lesson 68
Selection to be Memorized—"My Shadow"

Vocabulary:

notion—(noun) idea

arrant—(adjective) thorough

After reading the poem, have students answer the following questions. Use the memorization rubric to evaluate, page 108.

1. How many stanzas are in this poem?

   There are four stanzas in the poem.

2. Make a list of the words that rhyme.

   Words that rhyme are: me-see, head-bed, grow-slow, ball-all, play-way, see-me, up-buttercup, sleepyhead-bed.

3. **When is your shadow larger than you? When is it smaller than you?**
   Your shadow is larger than you when the sun is low in the east or low in the west (morning and late afternoon). Your shadow is smaller than you in the mid afternoon.
4. **Why is the shadow a coward?**
   The shadow is a coward because he always stays behind or beside you.
5. **When is the one time you cannot see your shadow.**
   You cannot see your shadow when there is no light.

Extended Activity

Focus a light on the student to make a shadow, then on a large piece of paper, have students trace their shadow. They can stand while someone else traces.

Lesson 69
Reproduction—Oral—"The Wind and the Sun"

Vocabulary—*quarrel*—(noun) an argument

Use the writing and dictation worksheet at the back of this book, page 118.

Lesson 70
Abbreviations

Jan.—January	Sun.—Sunday
Feb.—February	Mon.—Monday
Mar.—March	Tues.—Tuesday
Apr.—April	Wed.—Wednesday
Aug.—August	Thurs.—Thursday
Sept.—September	Fri.—Friday
Oct.—October	Sat.—Saturday
Nov.—November	Mr.—Mister
Dec.—December	Dr.—Doctor
St.—Street	Ave.—Avenue

In writing, words are sometimes shortened or abbreviated.
What mark of punctuation follows each abbreviation?
   Most abbreviations end in a period, one exception being the abbreviations for states and territories of the United States.
What is the abbreviation of the name of the state in which you live?
Name another state. What is the abbreviation?

Copy the below list.
Write the list from dictation.

Abbreviations of US States and Territories:

Alabama—AL
Alaska—AK
American Samoa—AS
Arizona—AZ
Arkansas—AR
California—CA
Colorado—CO
Connecticut—CT
Delaware—DE
District of Columbia—DC
Federated States of Micronesia—FM
Florida—FL
Georgia—GA
Guam—GU
Hawaii—HI
Idaho—ID
Illinois—IL
Indiana—IN
Iowa—IA
Kansas—KS
Kentucky—KY
Louisiana—LA
Maine—ME
Marshall Islands- MH
Maryland—MD
Massachusetts—MA
Michigan—MI
Minnesota—MN
Mississippi—MS
Missouri—MO

Montana—MT
Nebraska—NE
Nevada—NV
New Hampshire—NH
New Jersey—NJ
New Mexico—NM
New York—NY
North Carolina—NC
North Dakota—ND
Northern Mariana Islands—NP
Ohio—OH
Oklahoma—OK
Oregon—OR
Palau—PW
Pennsylvania—PA
Puerto Rico—PR
Rhode Island—RI
South Carolina—SC
South Dakota—SD
Tennessee—TN
Texas—TX
Utah—UT
Vermont—VT
Virgin Islands—VI
Virginia—VA
Washington—WA
West Virginia—WV
Wisconsin—WI
Wyoming—WY

Lesson 71
A Picture Story—
Lions at Home

How many lions can you see in the picture?
   There are five lions in the picture.
Which is the father lion?
   The father lion is the big lion with the heavy mane.
Which is the mother lion?
   The mother lion is the lion beside the father lion.
What do the little ones remind you of?
   The little lions remind one of kittens.
What is the artist's name?
   The artist's name is Rosa Bonheur.

Lesson 72
For Dictation

I am a lion. I live far away in Africa. In many ways I am like a cat. I have sharp teeth and sharp
   claws. I have cushions on my feet so that I can walk softly. I can see as well at night as in the
   daytime.
I hunt for my prey and spring upon it.
I am called the "King of Beasts."

Use the writing and dictation worksheet at the back of this book, page 118.

Lesson 73
Composition

Write a story that a horse might tell about himself, if he could talk.

Use the writing and dictation worksheet at the back of this book, page 118. Use the story rubric at the back of this book, page 112, to evaluate this composition.

Lesson 74
Composition

Write a story in which you use these words:
Bessie Thomas
woods
bluebird
violets
lunch
Saturday
basket
squirrel
afternoon
Write a story in which you use these words:
Frank Wilson
owner
five dollars
pocketbook
reward
found
Use the writing and dictation worksheet at the back of this book, page 118. Use the story rubric at the back of this book, page 112, to evaluate this composition.

Lesson 75
Dates

What mark of punctuation is placed between the day of the month and the year?
A comma is placed between the day of the month and the year.
Write these dates from dictation, using the abbreviation for the name of the month.
Refer to page 44 of this guide, Lesson 70, for monthly abbreviations.

Lesson 76
Observation Lesson

Name four parts of a chair.

An arm rest, legs, seat and back are four parts of a chair.

Name five parts of a watch.

A second, minute, and hour hand are three parts of a watch. A watch also has a face and a band.

Name as many parts as you can of a street car.

A street car has a cable, seats, stairs, and wheels.

Name several parts of a wagon.

A wagon has a handle, rails, and wheels.

Name five parts of a clock.

A clock has second, minute, and hour hands. It has a pendulum, alarm bells, gears and a face.

Name four or more parts of a sewing machine.

A sewing machine has a foot pedal, a needle, a bobbin, and a presser foot.

Name four parts of a harness.

A harness has a bridle, breast collar, pad, and breeching. Other parts are throat lash, winkers/blinkers, browband, winkerstay, noseband, liverpool bit, curb chain (all part of the bridle); rein, rein terret, terret, pad, tug, bellyband, wither strap, neck strap, breastcollar, girth, trace (all part of the collar and pad); and crupper, loin strap, back strap, breeching strap, breeching, trace carrier (all part of the breeching).

Name as many parts as you can of an automobile.

An automobile has wheels, a steering wheel, a gear shift, turn signals, seatbelts, doors, a motor, an exhaust pipe, a gas tank, windshield wipers, etc.

Name six parts of a house.

Six parts of a house are the kitchen, dining room, living room, bathroom, garage, and bedroom.

Extended Activities

As a friendly competition, make a list of other items, like a radio, television, computer, and bicycle, and see how many parts students can name in a minute.

Lesson 77
Eat—Ate—Eaten

1. When did you eat your breakfast?
2. I ate it this morning.
3. I have eaten my lunch and must go to school.
4. Tom has eaten his lunch, too.
5. Nellie had eaten an apple before I came home.

What word is used before eaten in the third sentence?

have

What word is used before eaten in the fourth sentence?

has

What word is used before eaten in the fifth sentence?

had

Copy these sentences, filling the blanks with *eat*, *ate*, or *eaten*.

1. Why don't you <u>eat</u> more?
2. I <u>ate</u> a lunch before dinner, and I am not hungry.
3. I have <u>eaten</u> a peach and a banana.
4. What did the boy <u>eat</u> that made him sick?
5. He <u>ate</u> some green apples.
6. Have you <u>eaten</u> your lunch?
7. I <u>ate</u> it an hour ago.
8. Did you <u>eat</u> it at school?
9. I <u>ate</u> it in the yard under the trees.
10. I have <u>eaten</u> it there every day this fall.
11. In the winter the squirrels <u>eat</u> the nuts that they had gathered in the summer.
12. After they had <u>eaten</u> their dinner, they slept.

Lesson 78
Selection to be Memorized—"One, Two, Three"

Use the memorization rubric at the back of this book, page 108, to evaluate this lesson.

After reading the poem, have students answer the following questions:

1. How many stanzas are in the poem?

   ten
2. What is the rhyme scheme of each stanza?

   abcb
3. Explain how the old lady and the little boy were playing hide and seek.

   The old lady and the little boy were playing hide and seek in their imagination.
4. What games can you play while sitting still?

   I spy
5. What vowel sound do all the rhyming words have?

   They all have the long e sound—three, see, he, knee, tree, me, etc.

Extended Activity

1. Play the hide and seek game as the old lady and the little boy did.
2. Play a game of "I Spy." Find an object within the room where you are located and have the other person guess what object you have selected.

Lesson 79
For Dictation—"The Wind"

The wind blows the clouds.
It sails the ships upon the seas.
It dries the clothes on the line.
It makes the windmills pump water.
It scatters seeds.
It blows away dust and bad air.

Use the dictation worksheet at the back of this book, page 118.

Lesson 80
One and More than One

Write these words so that they will mean more than one:

apple	*apples*
lion	*lions*
boy	*boys*
doll	*dolls*
girl	*girls*
clock	*clocks*
rabbit	*rabbits*
hat	*hats*
squirrel	*squirrels*
car	*cars*
book	*books*
basket	*baskets*
chair	*chairs*
pencil	*pencils*
cow	*cows*
bird	*birds*
flower	*flowers*
tree	*trees*
sister	*sisters*
brother	*brothers*

What letter did you add to each of these to make it mean more than one?
    S

Lesson 81

Reproduction—Oral and Written— "The Fox and the Crow"

Draw a picture suggested by this story.

Lesson 82

One and More than One

Copy these words so that they will mean more than one:

fox	*foxes*
church	*churches*
match	*matches*
peach	*peaches*
dish	*dishes*
dress	*dresses*
bush	*bushes*
watch	*watches*

Lesson 83

Reproduction—Oral and Written—"Silk"

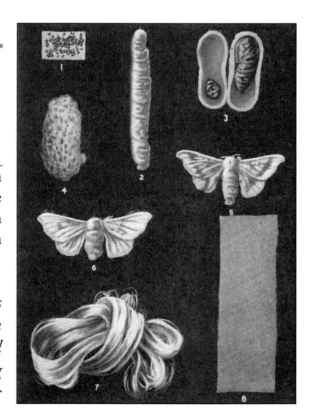

Extended Activity

Before introducing the lesson, have a piece of silk in class for the students to examine. Discuss where silk comes from and have students research and answer the following questions using an encyclopedia and/or the Internet.

1. When did the silk industry first begin?

   China was the first to cultivate silk about 5000 years ago. Later it spread to Korea, Japan and southern Asia. Centuries later silkworms were introduced to Europe and came to the United States during the 1800s, but the climate was not conducive for cultivation in this country and was discontinued.

2. **Where is silk manufactured today?**

  Have students locate China, Japan, France, Italy, and Spain on a globe, the major countries that cultivate silk today. Although silkworms are still used to produce silk, artificial fibers have replaced the use of silk in much of the textile industry.

3. **What do silkworms eat?**

  Silkworms feed off the mulberry tree. Artificial diets have also been developed to encourage their development. Answers:

Have the students read and/or write the story of reproduction on page 72.

Ask the students to retell the sequence of events in the story in their own words.

Have them research and explain each of the stages pictured on page 73.

Based on their research on the adult male (no. 5), have them draw and color a picture of the male moth. Adult moths have creamy white wings with brown patterns on the front wings.

This story includes many adjectives and nouns. Adjectives describe a noun, a person, place, thing, or idea. Adjectives make the story more interesting for the reader. List some of the adjectives and nouns used in this story.

Answers:

Adjective	Noun
pretty, white	moth
mulberry	tree
little	worms
green	leaves
soft, silken	covers
soft	threads
beautiful silk	cloth
big	ship
rich	merchant
little	girl

Have the students create an imaginary story from the perspective of a silkworm describing its life from egg to silk using at least five of the adjectives listed above to create their imaginary tale.

Lesson 84
Letter Writing

Write Henry's answer to Albert's letter, describing the knife and stating where he thought he lost it. Use the format shown for the correct way to write your response to Albert.

Use the letter writing rubric at the back of this book to evaluate this composition, page 114.

_____

                                                              date

Dear _____,

_____

_____

_____

_____

_____

_____

                                        Sincerely,

                                        _____

Lesson 85
One and More Than One

Copy these words, writing in one column the words that mean one, and in another column the words that mean more than one.

Words that mean one:
   foot, donkey, pony, mouse, lady, fly, cherry, goose, piano, child, knife, ox, man, woman
Words that mean more than one:
   ladies, mice, berries, feet, knives, men, teeth, turkeys, oxen, women, lilies, geese, ponies, children

One	More than One
foot	ladies
donkey	mice
pony	berries
mouse	feet
lady	knives
fly	men
cherry	teeth
goose	turkeys
piano	oxen
child	women
knife	lilies
ox	geese
man	ponies
woman	children

From your reader copy ten words that mean one and ten that mean more than one.

Have students review Lesson 83 on Reproduction to complete the above assignment.

Words that mean one from Lesson 83:

moth, tree, cloth, ship, sea, merchant, shop, lady, dress, girl

Words that mean more than one:

eggs, leaves, worms, they, covers, themselves, men, them, threads, machines

Lesson 86

Reading Lesson—Dialogue for Two Pupils

1. Who is it? It is I.
2. Did you knock at the door? No, it was not I; it was he.
3. Is that your brother? Yes, it is he.
4. Who called? It was I.
5. Who threw the snowballs? It was they.
6. Did Mary speak? I think it was she.
7. Who fell down? It was not I.
8. Who laughed? It was we.
9. Who was standing at the window? It was she.
10. Did Helen break her doll? No, it was I who broke it.
11. Is your cousin here? Yes, that is he.

Note to the teacher—This lesson should be repeated in many different recitations, until the forms no longer seem strange or unusual.

Extended Activities

Subject pronouns are as follows: *I, you, he, she, it, we, they*. Subject pronouns are used as the subject of the sentence and after the form of the verb be (*am, is, are, was, were, being, been*) when they repeat the subject as in this dialogue.

Have the students write the dialogue on flash cards, the question on one side, the answer on the back. Student one can flash the question and student two can answer with the appropriate response as written on the back of the card held by student one.

Have students create new dialogues with which to practice the correct use of subject nouns.

Lesson 87
Choice of Words

Choose words from the list below to fill blanks in the following sentences.

on, to, by, above, around, into, at, in, for, under, across, after

Answers
1. The book is <u>on</u> the table.
2. The pencil is on the floor <u>under</u> the table.
3. Nellie lives <u>across</u> the street.
4. Is your mother <u>at</u> home?
5. I think she has gone <u>to</u> the concert.
6. We threw sticks <u>into</u> the water, and Rover went after them.
7. Is Frank <u>in</u> the house?
8. The blue sky is <u>above</u> us.
9. The air is <u>around</u> us.

Extended Activity

These words are prepositions, words that show position, direction, or how two words are related to each other. The most common prepositions are: *about, above, across, after, against, along, among, around, at, before, behind, below, beneath, beside, between, beyond, by, down, from, in, inside, into, like, near, off, on, onto, out, outside, over, past, through, throughout, to, toward, under, underneath, until, upon, with, and within.*

Give students a list of these prepositions, along with a Styrofoam cup, 10 toothpicks, and 10 sticky tabs per student. Have them create a preposition mobile by finding ten prepositions from the list and writing one on each sticky tab. Place the tab on the toothpick and stick the toothpick in the cup according to the preposition listed, i.e., on the cup, inside the cup, through the cup.

Lesson 88

Whose?

A possessive noun shows ownership. The possessive form of singular nouns is usually shown by adding an *'s* to the noun that possesses an object.

1. The desk belonging to the teacher is at the front of the room.
2. The teacher's desk is at the front of the room.
3. The nest of the little bird is at the top of the tree.
4. The little bird's nest is at the top of the tree.

Is there any difference in the meaning between the first and second sentences?

No, the sentence meanings are the same.

What does *'s* added to the word *teacher* show?

The 's shows that the teacher owns the desk.

Is there any difference in the meaning between the third and fourth sentences?

No, the sentence meanings are the same.

What does *'s* added to the word *bird* show?

The 's shows that the bird owns the nest.

Write these sentences from dictation:

1. Nellie's new dress was torn.
2. The dog's master went away on the train.
3. Tom's book has beautiful pictures in it.
4. Mr. White's horse ran away.
5. Did you see Frank's little pony?

Use the writing and dictation worksheet at the back of this book, page 118.

Lesson 89

Copy these sentences and fill the blanks with words that answer the question, *Whose?* Answers may vary but should reflect the correct use of the *'s* with singular nouns.

1. The *child's* playthings were on the floor.
2. The poor *boy's* coat was ragged.
3. Uncle *Bob's* farm is near the city.
4. A *snake's* bite is poisonous.
5. *Jen's* skates were bright and new.
6. The *sun's* light is very bright.
7. The lazy *man's* work was not finished.
8. *Tom's* father is sick.
9. The *bird's* song is sweet.

10. The fox stole the *mouse's* cheese.
11. The *goat's* little ones are called kids.
12. The *cat's* little ones are called kittens.
13. The *dog's* little ones are called puppies.

Extended Activity

Have the student select the correct form of the possessive noun in the following sentences. The correct answers are italicized for the teacher.

1. The _____ tail was fluffy and soft.
   a. squirrel's
   b. squirrels
   c. squirrels'
2. The _____ bone fell into the mud.
   a. dogs
   b. dogs'
   c. dog's
3. _____ car ran out of gas.
   a. Mother's
   b. Mothers
   c. Mothers'
4. My _____ pet bird can talk.
   a. friends
   b. friends'
   c. friend's
5. The _____ voice was too soft.
   a. teachers'
   b. teacher's
   c. teachers
6. The _____ noise scared the child.
   a. thunders
   b. thunder's
   c. thunders'
7. A _____ teeth are very sharp.
   a. shark's
   b. sharks'
   c. sharks
8. The _____ face was painted red.
   a. clowns
   b. clown's
   c. clowns'
9. The _____ tail fluttered in the breeze.
   a. kites
   b. kites'
   c. kite's

10. My _____ room is always clean.
    a. sister's
    b. sisters'
    c. sisters

Lesson 90

Use these words in sentences.
Harry's, dog's, father's, Edith's, horse's, children's, Mr. Smith's, rabbit's, squirrel's

Extended Activity

Have the students make a chart showing possessive nouns. The left column should be supplied to
    the students as shown below, then the student should fill in the correct form on the right.

Answers:

the sweater of John	*John's sweater*
the bike of Susan	*Susan's bike*
the nest of the bird	*bird's nest*
the bark of the dog	*dog's bark*
the bite of the spider	*spider's bite*
the sting of the bee	*bee's sting*
the tail of the horse	*horse's tail*
the milk of the cow	*cow's milk*
the neck of the dinosaur	*dinosaur's neck*
the eggs of the hen	*hen's eggs*

the sweater of John

the bike of Susan's

the nest of the bird

the bark of the dog

the bite of the spider

the sting of the bee

the tail of the horse

the milk of the cow

the neck of the dinosaur

the eggs of the hen

Lesson 91

Selection to Be Memorized— "The Wonderful World"

Extended Activity

After the student has read the poem, answer the following questions.

1. In Lesson 83, page 52 in this guide, you learned about adjectives. The poet used many adjectives in describing the world. List as many different adjectives as you can find.

   Possible answers include: great, wide, wonderful, beautiful, friendly, white, small

2. The poet describes many places and things in his poem. In Lesson 83 you learned that nouns are persons, places, things, or ideas. How many nouns can you find in this poem?

   Possible answers include; world, water, grass, air, wind, tree, mills, hills, earth, fields, rivers, cities, gardens, oceans, isles, people, miles, prayers, mother, father

Have students make a nature collage showing the various places the poet mentioned in his poem.

List the pairs of rhyming words in the poem.

   world, curled; breast, dressed; me, tree; mills, hills; go, flow; isles, miles; small, all; today, gay; you, too; dot, cannot

Lesson 92

Go—Went—Gone

1. I go to school every day.
2. I went to the country last summer.
3. Mother has gone to Chicago.
4. The girls have gone home.
5. I called for you this morning, but you had gone.
6. I think that all the children have gone.

What word is used before *gone* in the third sentence?

   The word has *is used before gone.*

What word is used before *gone* in the fourth sentence?

   The word have is used before gone.

What word is used before *gone* in the fifth sentence?

   The word had *is used before gone.*

In the sixth sentence?

   The word have *is used.*

Copy these sentences and fill the blanks with *go, went,* or *gone.*
1. We <u>go</u> to school five days in the week.
2. Fred <u>went</u> to the country last summer.
3. The birds have <u>gone</u> to the warm South land.
4. When spring comes, the snow will <u>go</u> away.
5. Nellie's big brother has <u>gone</u> away to school.
6. The children <u>went</u> to the park last summer.
7. The boys have <u>gone</u> across the street to play ball.
8. The girls took their dolls and <u>went</u> down by the river.
9. Rover has <u>gone</u> with Frank after the cows.
10. The birds will return when the snow has <u>gone</u> away.
11. Wynken, Blynken, and Nod <u>went</u> off in a wooden shoe.
12. They had not <u>gone</u> far when they saw the moon.

Lesson 93

Reproduction—Oral— "The Lion and the Mouse"

Extended Activity

The comprehension questions should be answered orally after reading the passage.
1. **What caused the lion to wake up?**
   A little mouse ran across his face and woke him.
2. **What did the lion plan to do with the mouse?**
   He was going to kill the mouse.
3. **How did the mouse save herself from being killed?**
   She begged so hard for her life, the lion released her.
4. **What happened to the lion after that?**
   He was caught in a trap.
5. **How did the lion escape the trap?**
   The little mouse nibbled through the cords and freed the lion.
6. **How did the lion feel after he was set free?**
   He was glad he saved the life of the little mouse.
7. **What lesson does this little tale teach us?**
   Accept any reasonable answer such as: It teaches us that kindness always pays; we're never too small to help another person in trouble.

Lesson 94
Composition

Copy what the lion says and supply what the mouse says. Accept any reasonable answer.

Lion: Something woke me up. I wonder what it was. Here is something under my paw. Why, it
    is a mouse! Why did you wake me up?
Mouse:
Lion: I am going to eat you.
Mouse:
Lion: Why should I let you go?
Mouse:
Lion: I will let you go this time, but don't wake me again.

Use the writing and dictation worksheets at the back of this book, page 118.

Lesson 95
Conversation Lesson

Extended Activity
Tell something about each article of food, where it was obtained, and who had to work before it
    was ready to be eaten.

Possible Answers:
    *The articles of food mentioned in the story are oatmeal, cream, sugar, beefsteak, pepper, salt,
    buttered toast, cocoa. The foods were obtained from plants, minerals, and animals.*
    Plants: oatmeal (grain), sugar, pepper, toast (wheat), cocoa
    Minerals: salt
    Animals: cream, beefsteak, butter

Have the students research each item to see how it was gathered and processed for
    consumption.

Lesson 96
Contractions

doesn't	I'm
aren't	isn't
weren't	couldn't
wouldn't	we'll
hasn't	they'll
haven't	can't
o'clock	didn't
shouldn't	don't
they're	it's

Of what two words is each of the words composed? What mark shows that a letter or letters have been omitted?

A contraction is composed by shortening a word, a syllable, or a word group, omitting a sound or letter and adding an apostrophe in its place. The apostrophe is used to indicate a missing letter/letters.

Copy the list, writing after each word its equivalent.

Contraction	Written Out	Letter Replaced by Apostrophe
doesn't	*does not*	*o*
I'm	*I am*	*a*
aren't	*are not*	*o*
isn't	*is not*	*o*
weren't	*were not*	*o*
couldn't	*could not*	*o*
wouldn't	*would not*	*o*
we'll	*we will*	*wi*
hasn't	*has not*	*o*
they'll	*they will*	*wi*
haven't	*have not*	*o*
can't	*can not*	*no*
o'clock	*of the clock*	*f the*
didn't	*did not*	*o*
shouldn't	*should not*	*o*
don't	*do not*	*o*
they're	*they are*	*a*
it's	*it is*	*i*

Extended Activity

Choose any ten of the contractions land use them correctly in sentences.

Lesson 97
Words Opposite in Meaning

In column 2, find a word opposite in meaning to each word in column 1. Copy the words in
  pairs; thus, hot—cold.

Column 1	Column 2
black	difficult
hot	bad
slow	low
hard	ugly
sour	dry
narrow	soft
short	cold
dark	fast
late	white
straight	poor
wet	noisy
beautiful	big
high	rough
good	wide
smooth	sweet
well	old
little	long
new	tall
rich	crooked
easy	light
quiet	sick
thick	early
short	thin

Answers

black—white
hot—cold
slow—fast
hard—soft
sour—sweet
narrow—wide
short—tall
dark—light
late—early
straight—crooked
wet—dry
beautiful—ugly

high—low
good—bad
smooth—rough
well—sick
little—big
new—old
rich—poor
easy—difficult
quiet—noisy
thick—thin
short—long

Lesson 98

Composition

Use in sentences the first ten words of column 1 on page 85.
Sentences should include the following words:

black, hot, slow, hard, sour, narrow, short, dark, late, straight.

Use the writing and dictation worksheet at the back of this book, page 118.

Lesson 99

Composition

Answer the following questions in complete sentences.

What is your name?
How old are you?
Have you any brothers and sisters? If so, tell their names.
Where do you go to school?
How long have you been going to school?
What grade are you in?
How many pupils are there in your class?
What study do you like best?
What do you play after school and on Saturdays?
What games do you like best?
What work can you do?

Lesson 100

Reproduction—
"The Humming Bird and the Butterfly"

Tell what you know of the change of a caterpillar to a butterfly.

Extended Activity

Students may illustrate and identify each of the stages of the development of a butterfly using
the chart. Stages should include the egg, the larva or caterpillar, the pupa, and the adult.
Have the student tell of a time when someone was kind to them or they were kind to someone else.

Stage 1—_____

Stage 2—_____

_____

_____

_____

Stage 3—_____

Stage 4—_____

_____

_____

Color this butterfly.

Lesson 101

Write an account of a conversation between a rabbit and a squirrel. Use the same form as that given in Lesson 100. Be sure to include a moral in your story, some lesson we can learn from the rabbit and the squirrel.

Use the writing and dictation worksheet at the back of this book, page 118.

Lesson 102
A Picture Lesson—
Two Mothers

Answers may vary.

What do you see in the picture?

In the picture you see a mother carrying her baby and a mother cow walking beside her baby calf.

How does the mother show that she loves her baby?

The mother shows that she loves her baby by the smile on her face and by dressing the baby warmly.

Does a cow love her calf? How does she show it?

A mother cow shows her love for her baby by providing milk for her calf.

How does a cat show her love for her kittens?

A mother cat licks her kittens to clean and dry them. Mother cats nurse their babies and protect them from predators.

What will a mother dog do if her babies are hurt?

A mother dog will lick her babies' wounds and protect them from attackers.

What other animals have you seen that showed love for their young ones?

Answers will vary.

How does a mother bird care for her little ones?

A mother bird provides juicy insects or other types of food that contain moisture for her little birds until they are old enough to fly and leave the nest.

What is the name of the picture?

This picture is titled Two Mothers. *It is also known as* Motherhood.

Write a story about the picture.

Teacher Notes

This painting was done by French artist Edouard-Bernard Debat-Ponsan (1847-1913). He studied in Toulouse which still has a large collection of his works. His art work includes historical paintings as well as religious works. He is known for his brilliant colors and vivid details, as seen in this work of art.

Extended Activity

Have the students identify the details that Debat-Ponsan puts in his work by answering the following questions.

1. **What two families do you see in this picture?**

    The artist shows a mother and child and a cow and her calf.

2. **Is the mother wealthy or poor?**

    She is probably poor. She and her child are barefooted and her apron seems to be patched. She is dressed like a peasant.

3. **The two mothers seem to feel contented to be together. How might the cow and the calf help the woman and her child?**

    The cow provides milk, butter, and cheese for the family. The calf may provide more food when it is grown, or it may be sold to get other supplies needed by the family.

4. **How might the mother help the cow and her calf?**

    She might provide them shelter, food, and water.

5. **What do you notice about the cow and calf's hooves?**

    In a dictionary look up the word cloven: a foot divided into two parts.

6. **What other details can you find in the picture that show the artist's skill in drawing?**

Lesson 103
Observation Lesson—Tools

Answers to questions may vary.

What tool does the carpenter use?

   A carpenter may use levels, saws, hammers, nails, measuring tapes, planers, saw horses, screwdrivers.

What tools does the blacksmith use?

   A blacksmith may use anvils, tongs, hammers, nails.

What tools does the shoemaker use?

   A shoemaker may use knives, hammers, awls.

What tools does a stone mason use?

   A mason may use hammers, chisels, stone cutters, sledges, levels, trowels.

What tools and machinery does a farmer use?

   A farmer may use tractors, plows, balers, combines, scythes, augers, hammers.

What tools does a dentist use?

   A dentist may use tooth scrapers, picks, syringes, pliers, gloves, masks.

What tools does a woman use in cooking?

   A woman may use pots, pans, knives, graters, choppers, spatulas, scrapers.

What tools do you use in your work at school?

   A student may use pencils, paper, erasers, computers, scissors, staplers, glue.

Extended Activity

Have students research the various kinds of tools needed for each of these jobs, either in an encyclopedia or on the Internet. Students can draw and label the tools and explain how they are used. Students can also create a collage of tools needed for the various jobs.

Lesson 104
Selection to be Memorized—"November"

The parts into which this poem is divided are called stanzas. How many stanzas are in this poem?

This poem has seven stanzas.

With what kind of letter does each stanza begin?

Each stanza begins with a capital letter.

Copy the first stanza.

The first stanza is:
> *The leaves are fading and falling,*
> *The winds are rough and wild,*
> *The birds have ceased their calling,*
> *But let me tell you, my child,*

Copy two words that describe roses.

Bright and red describe the roses.

Copy two words that describe blossoms.

Loveliest and wayside describe the blossoms.

Copy one word that describes leaves.

New describes the leaves.

Copy two words that describe the wind.

Rough and wild describe the wind.

Copy two words that describe weather.

Rough and cold describe the weather.

Who wrote this poem?

Alice Cary wrote this poem.

Extended Activity

Have the students identify the rhyming pattern and list the rhyming words in each stanza; every other line rhymes.

The rhyming words are: falling—calling; wild—child; closes—roses; grow—snow; over—clover; leaves—eaves; bosom—blossoms; new—dew; whirling—darling; dumb—come; weather—together; wild—child; loses—rose; glow—snow.

Poets frequently use alliteration in their poems, words with the same beginning consonant sounds. Alice Cary uses alliteration in each stanza. Have the students find and list the alliterative words.

Stanza 1: fading falling; Stanza 2: day day doth darker; red roses; Stanza 3: when winter will will Stanza 4: will wear will with; Stanza 5: dry dumb darling Stanza 6: weather winds wild; Stanza 7 roots roses.

Lesson 105

Fill these blanks with words from the list at the end of the lesson.
1. An owl cannot *sing*.
2. We *sang* in school yesterday.
3. The teacher *rang* the bell at nine o'clock.
4. The goldenrod *grew* in the woods last fall.
5. We have *sung* that song many times.
6. Did you hear me *ring* the bell?
7. I have *rung* it many times.
8. How tall that tree has *grown*!
9. I *knew* you would come.
10. Do you *know* your lesson?
11. I have *known* you a long time.
12. Every year I *grow* taller.

Extended Activity

Choose the correct form of the word to complete each sentence.
1. ring: When I hear my alarm clock *ring*, I know I have to get up.
2. sing: Every morning when I get up, I hear birds *sing* outside my window.
3. know: I *know* I will be late for school if I sleep in.
4. grow: If I want to *grow* smarter, I have to study hard.
5. grow: I *grew* two inches this past year.
6. ring: My cell phone *rang* in class yesterday.
7. sing: We have *sung* the national anthem every year at our parade.
8. know: I *knew* it by heart when I was only 5 years old.
9. sing: I even *sang* it alone in front of my kindergarten class.
10. ring: The melody has *rung* in my ears all morning.
11. know: It is a well-*known* hymn in America.
12. grow: It has *grown* to become a national symbol of our country.

Lesson 106

Reproduction—Oral and Written—"An Acorn"

Read this story, close your books, and write the story from memory.
Draw a picture suggested by this lesson.

Extended Activity

Have students write a creative story pretending to be the acorn from the time it was planted until
   children move into the house it helped to build. Students should include the 5 W's: *who,
   what, when, where, why.* Also include in their stories the five senses: what did the acorn see,
   feel, hear, smell, taste? See the essay rubric at the back of this book, page 113, for grading.

Lesson 107

Most—Almost

1. It is almost five o'clock.
2. Which boy has the most money?
3. I think Frank has the most.
4. My work is almost done.

In which of the above sentences can *nearly* be used instead of the underlined word?
   Nearly can be used in sentence 1 and sentence 4.

Copy these sentences and fill the blanks with almost or most.
   1. Harry is *almost* as tall as Charles.
   2. *Most* of the birds go south in winter.
   3. The lion *almost* caught the deer.
   4. Nellie is *almost* nine years old.
   5. *Most* children like to play.
   6. The man *almost* missed the train.
   7. *Most* trees shed their leaves in the fall.
Copy from your readers two sentences that contain the word *almost.* Copy two sentences that
   contain the word *most.*

Lesson 108
Observation Lesson

What direction is opposite of south?
North is opposite of south.
What direction is opposite of west?
East is opposite of west.
What direction is opposite of north?
South is opposite of north.
What direction is opposite of east?
West is opposite of east.
What direction is between north and east?
Northeast is between north and east.
What direction is between north and west?
Northwest is between north and west.
What direction is between south and east?
Southeast is between south and east.
What direction is between south and west?
Southwest is between south and west.
In what direction is your home from the school?
Answers will vary.
Mention something that is north of the schoolhouse.
Answers will vary.
Mention something that is west of your home.
Answers will vary.

Extended Activity

In small groups have students create a scavenger hunt for other students to locate objects on the school ground. Students should use at least six of the directions in the list of directions.

Supply each group a map of their state or city. Have them find towns located on the map using the directions listed in the questions.

Lesson 109
For Dictation—"Insects"

An insect has six legs. The body of an insect is divided into three parts. On its head are two long feelers, called antennae. Many insects have two or four wings.

Some insects live in the air, some make their homes in the earth, and some live in the water.

Answers will vary.
Name six insects.
Write sentences, telling something about each of the six insects.

Lesson 110
Reproduction—Oral—"The Fox and the Grapes"

One day a fox saw some grapes at the top of a high grapevine. He was thirsty, and he thought how good the juicy grapes would taste.

He jumped and tried to reach them, but he could not. He tried again and again, but in vain.

At last he said, "I don't care; I don't want them. I know they are sour grapes."

Into how many parts is this story divided?
The story is divided into three parts.
What does the first part tell about?
The first part tells about a fox who was thirsty, and he found some juicy grapes.
What does the second part tell about?
The second part tells how he tried to reach the grapes, but he couldn't because they were too high on the vine.
What does the third part tell about?
The third part tells how he gave up and tried to convince himself that the grapes weren't good anyway.
Each of these parts is a paragraph.

How many paragraphs are there in the story?
The story has three paragraphs.
What shows the beginning of a paragraph?
Beginning a new line, indenting the first word and capitalizing the first letter shows a new paragraph.
Write the first two paragraphs of this story from dictation.
The first two paragraphs are:
One day a fox saw some grapes at the top of a high grapevine. He was thirsty, and he thought how good the juicy grapes would taste.
He jumped and tried to reach them, but he could not. He tried again and again, but in vain.
Draw a picture suggested by this story.

Extended Activity

What moral does this little story teach us?

It teaches us not to give up or pout if we can't get what we want.

Describe a time when you or someone you know behaved like the fox, using three paragraphs that start a new line, indent, and use a capital letter at the beginning of each paragraph.

Lesson 111
A Picture Lesson—
"You're No Chicken"

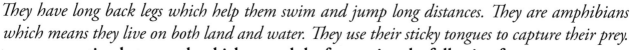

What do you see in the picture?

Two little chicks are inspecting a frog.

Tell what you know about frogs.

Answers will vary but may include the following ideas. Frogs are small animals without tails or necks. Their bulging eyes can see in almost all directions.

They have long back legs which help them swim and jump long distances. They are amphibians which means they live on both land and water. They use their sticky tongues to capture their prey.

Write a conversation between the chickens and the frog, using the following form:

Chicken: _____

Frog: _____

Chicken: _____

Frog: _____

Let the chickens ask the questions and the frog reply, telling things about himself.

Lesson 112
Observation Lesson—Oral—Spiders

How many legs has a spider?

A spider has eight legs.

How many legs has a fly? An ant? A bee?

A fly has six legs. An ant has six legs. A bee has six legs.

Into how many parts is the body of the spider divided?

The body of the spider is divided into two main sections: the cephalothorax (head and thorax) is joined to the abdomen by the pedicel, or thin waist.

Into how many parts are the bodies of the ant and the bee divided?

The ant is divided into three parts: the head, the trunk and the metasoma. The bee is divided into three parts: the head, the thorax (chest) and the abdomen.

What does the spider spin?

The spider spins a silk web.

What is the purpose of spinning the web?

The web catches insects for the spider's food.

When a fly or other insect is caught in the web, what does the spider do?

The spider attacks the insect and eats it.

Where does the spider place its eggs?

Most spiders place their eggs in an egg sac made of a special kind of silk. Some spiders die after the eggs are laid; others stay with the egg sacs until they hatch.

Read the questions silently; answer in complete statements.

Draw a spider's web, showing the spider in the center of it.

Extended Activity

Have the students research a spider, a bee, and an ant. Complete a chart by explaining how each one is valuable and harmful to humans.

Benefits	Detriments
Spiders eat harmful insects which threaten crops or carry diseases.	*Spiders, bees and ants all have the potential for biting/stinging.*
Ants eat harmful insects that may destroy crops or other vegetation. When they dig their nests underground, they break up the soil and loosen it to absorb more water and make it less hard-packed.	*Ants can also be agricultural pests that protect harmful insects. They can damage homes by burrowing through wooden beams; they eat household food that is not properly covered and become pests at picnics.*
Bees (honey bees) provide us with honey for both cooking and as a sweet spread on bread. They also provide beeswax for making candles, polishes and even some lipsticks. They fertilize flowers of fruits and vegetables that help them produce good crops.	

Lesson 113

Conversation and Reproduction—
"The Ostrich"

Write a short composition, telling all you can about ostriches.

Extended Activity
Have the students complete a chart which will provide notes for their composition.

size _____

color _____

speed _____

unique features _____

defense mechanisms _____

food _____

value to humans _____

From the information found in the story and their research, the student should include the following information in the composition.

Ostriches stand about 8 feet tall and weigh up to 345 pounds. It is the only bird with two toes on each foot. The male ostrich has black and white feathers; the female's feathers are brown.

The ostrich cannot fly, but it can run very fast, up to 40 miles per hour in short bursts, which helps it escape from its predators. It will kick its legs or attack with its toe nails if it is cornered. The male ostrich's voice has a deep roar with a hissing sound. An ostrich's food consists of plants, lizards, and turtles. It also eats sand and gravel to help grind its food for better digestion. Ostriches can live for long periods of time without water. Over the years ostriches were hunted for their plumes, used in decorating. Today they are mostly hunted for their skin which is used for fine leather products. See the rubric for writing an essay, page 113.

In America we have a saying that if we're in trouble, we may bury our heads in the sand like the ostrich.

True or false: Does an ostrich bury its head in the sand when frightened?

The answer is false. No one has ever seen an ostrich with its head in the sand. When in danger it may lay its head and neck close to the ground, thus blending into its habitat.

Lesson 114
Selection to be Memorized

He prayeth best who loveth best
    All things both great and small;
For the dear God who loveth us,
    He made and loveth all.
        Samuel Taylor Coleridge

Write the above quotation from memory. See rubric for oral reading/memorization at the back of this book for evaluation, page 108 and 111.

Lesson 115
Reproduction—Oral and Written— "Moth and Butterfly"

Into how many paragraphs is this selection divided?
    This selection is divided into four paragraphs.
What does each paragraph tell?
    Paragraph one describes the antennae of the butterfly and the moth.
    Paragraph two explains where the butterfly and moth place their wings while resting.
    Paragraph three tells when they fly, the butterfly in the daytime and the moth at night.
    Paragraph four states the difference in their body weight; the moth is heavier than the butterfly.
Write this selection from memory, using the same number of paragraphs.

Lesson 116
Letter Writing

Copy the letter. Write the letter from dictation. Use the writing and dictation worksheet, page 118.

Lesson 117
Letter Writing

Write Helen's answer to Ethel's letter, stating that she could not get *Black Beauty,* but is sending her another book. Tell the name of the book and something about it. Helen hopes that Ethel will soon be well.

Use this letter layout as a guide.

Use the letter writing rubric at the back of this book for evaluation.

```
                                              HEADING

         SALUTATION,




                             BODY




                          CLOSING,

                          SIGNATURE
```

Lesson 118
Exclamation Point

Read the first stanza of "The Swing" in Lesson 28. The mark after the fourth line is an exclamation point.

How do you like to go up in a swing,
    Up in the air so blue?
Oh, I do think it the pleasantest thing,
    Ever a child can do!

How many other exclamation points can you find in the poem?

The last line in the last stanza also has an exclamation point. Up in the air and down!

Read the poem, "The Brown Thrush," Lesson 46. Copy the parts that are followed by exclamation points.

He's singing to me! He's singing to me!
    Oh, the world's running over with joy!
Hush! Look! In my tree,
    I'm as happy as happy can be!
Don't meddle! Don't touch!
    Or the world will lose some of its joy!
Now I'm glad! Now I'm free!
    Oh, the world's running over with joy!

Find ten exclamation points in your reader. Copy the words or sentences that are followed by these points.

From the textbook, Lesson 119: "The Bluebird," contains seven exclamation points as follows. Brave little fellow! Hark! how the music leaps out from his throat! Hark! Little white snowdrop! Daffodils! Daffodils!

Lesson 119
Selection to be Memorized—"The Bluebird"

Extended Activity

In this poem the poet uses personification, giving non-human things human characteristics. He is talking to the bluebird and flowers as if they were people. What human things does he ask the bluebird and flowers to do?

The bluebird will "sing you a message of cheer." He tells the snowdrop, "I pray you arise." To the crocus he says, "Come, open your eyes." To the violets he says, "Put on your mantles of purple and gold." And to the daffodils he says, "Say, do you hear?"

Research the four types of flowers and learn where and when they grow. Then create a piece of art that shows the bluebird and flowers performing the human characteristics he describes. Be sure to use the bright colors described by the poet in your art work.

Lesson 120
Composition

A robin has been down South all winter; he has just returned to some place near your home. He and his mate are looking for a place to build a nest.

Write a story that the robin might tell if he could talk. Begin your story in this way: "A Robin's Story" I have just returned from the South. I am a little tired from flying so far, but I am glad to be back again. Include in your story the 5 W's: who, what, when where, and why. Use lots of descriptive words that appeal to the reader's sense of sight, sound, touch, smell, and/or taste.

Use the essay rubric at the back of this book for evaluation, page 113.

Lesson 121
Quotations and Quotation Marks

What are the exact words that Will said?

Will's exact words are, "Let us go to the pond and fish."

Repeat the exact words of the mother.

Mother's exact words are, "Yes, you may go, and here is something nice for your lunch."

When the exact words of another are repeated, these words are called a direct quotation. The marks (" ") that enclose a direct quotation are called *quotation marks*.

What other mark of punctuation is placed after the direct quotation in the first sentence?

In the first sentence a comma is used after the direct quotation.

In the second sentence?

In the second sentence a comma is used after the direct quotation.

In the third sentence?

In the third sentence a comma is used after the direct quotation.

Where are the commas used in the fourth sentence?

In the fourth sentence the comma is used before the direct quotation, after the interjection (yes), and between the compound sentences (you may go, and here is something nice for your lunch.").

Write the above conversation from dictation.

Extended Activity

For additional practice have students edit the following sentences for correct use of quotation marks and commas.

1. I'm hungry George moaned.

    "I'm hungry," George moaned.

2. What are you hungry for? asked Mother.

    "What are you hungry for?" asked Mother.

3. Pepperoni pizza and coke George responded.

    "Pepperoni pizza and coke," George responded.

4. Mother replied We had that last night for dinner.

    Mother replied, "We had that last night for dinner."

5. **Were there any leftovers? George asked.**

   "Were there any leftovers?" George asked.

6. **Yes you're in luck Mother answered. Go raid the fridge and clean up the dishes when you're finished she added.**

   "Yes, you're in luck," Mother answered. "Go raid the fridge, and clean up the dishes when you're finished," she added.

Lesson 122

For Dictation—"The Hare and the Tortoise"

Use the writing and dictation worksheets at the back of this book, page 118.

Lesson 123

For Dictation—
"The Hare and the Tortoise" (Continued)

Use the writing and dictation worksheets at the back of this book, page 118.

Extended Activity

(After reading Lessons 122-123, pages 106-107 in the textbook.)
Read the sentences below then number them 1-8 to show the sequence of the events.

"Slow as I am, I can beat you," replied the tortoise.
But when he reached the big tree the tortoise was there waiting for him.
The hare went a little way and then lay down and took a nap.
"Slow and steady wins the race," said the tortoise.
"You think you can beat me, do you?" said the hare.
"What a slow fellow you are!" said a hare to a tortoise.
By and by he awoke and ran as fast as he could.
The tortoise started at once and kept straight on.

1. *"What a slow fellow you are!" said a hare to a tortoise.*
2. *"Slow as I am, I can beat you," replied the tortoise.*
3. *"You think you can beat me, do you?" said the hare.*
4. *The tortoise started at once and kept straight on.*
5. *The hare went a little way and then lay down and took a nap.*
6. *By and by he awoke and ran as fast as he could.*

7. But when he reached the big tree the tortoise was there waiting for him.

8. "Slow and steady wins the race," said the tortoise.

Lesson 124

Reproduction—Oral and Written
An Indian Myth—"The Origin of the Birds"

Extended Activity

A myth is a story that attempts to explain some mystery of nature. It often contains gods and goddesses with superhuman actions, like this Indian myth. Think of a natural phenomenon such as hurricanes if you live in a coastal area or tornadoes or earthquakes if you live in an area that experiences those acts of nature. Create a myth that explains how it began. When and where did it first occur? Who was there? What did they say or do? What was the result of this phenomenon?

Lesson 125

Selection for Study—
"Who Made the Stars?"

How many words in this poem refer to God?

The poet refers to God in eight different words: God, Glorious One, He, His, He, Him, Father, Friend.

With what kind of letter does each of these words begin?

Each word referring to God begins with a capital letter.

How many stanzas are there in this poem?

This poem has three stanzas.

Which lines in each stanza are indented?

The second and fourth lines in each stanza are indented.

Extended Activity

An *inference* is drawing a reasonable conclusion about an event based on what you have seen or read. The writer does not state exactly all the details but depends on the reader to make an "educated guess" about the situation. In Lesson 121, you learned about quotation marks and when they should be used. In this poem, each stanza begins and ends with quotation marks meaning each stanza has a specific speaker.

Who is speaking in the first stanza, and what words help you know that?

In this poem the poet uses specific words to show who is speaking in the first two stanzas. In the third stanza the reader must make an inference about who is speaking. The first stanza begins with "Mother" indicating a child is talking.

Who is speaking in the second stanza and what words help you know that?

The second stanza uses the words "my child" to show the mother is talking.

Who is speaking in the third stanza and what words help you know that?

The third stanza does not use a specific word to indicate who the speaker is, but since the words are a continuation of what the Mother wants to teach the child, we can infer that Mother is still speaking.

Mother	Child

"'Twas God, my child, the Glorious One.
  He formed them by His power;
He made alike the brilliant sun,
  and every leaf and flower."
 	
"In all the changing scenes of time,
  On Him our hopes depend;
In every age, in every clime,
  Our Father and our friend."
	"Mother, who made the stars which light
	  The beautiful blue sky?
	Who made the moon, so clear and bright,
	  That rises up so high?"

Lesson 126
A Picture Lesson—
Soap Bubbles

What do you see in the picture?

What are the children doing? Tell how to make soap bubbles.

Write a story about the picture, telling the names of the children, who the oldest girl is, how old the younger ones are, and what grade they are in at school. Tell what time of year it is. Add other items to your story.

About the Artist

Elizabeth Gardner was an American artist who painted at the turn of the twentieth century. She was born in Exeter, New Hampshire, and grew up in a cultured family, surrounded by art and literature.

In her twenties, Elizabeth went to Paris to study painting and soon learned that Parisian schools of art were not admitting women. Because of illness, her hair had been cut short before leaving the United States, so she posed as a boy and was accepted at France's great drawing school in the Gobelin Tapestry Factory.

She was the first woman to exhibit a painting at the Paris Salon of the French Academy of Art, as well as the first American woman to receive a gold medal from the Academy.

Elizabeth's professor at Gobelin was William Adolphe Bouguereau, a well-known painter. He was a widower with two children and eventually married Elizabeth.

She was later instrumental in founding the School of Design in Worcester, Mass.

Soap Bubbles, one of her most famous paintings, was exhibited in the department of Fine Arts for the United States at the World's Columbian Exposition in 1893. The Library in the Jefferson Hotel, opened in 1896, still houses *Soap Bubbles.* At least forty of Elizabeth's other paintings still exist.

Elizabeth Gardner Bouguereau dared to challenge old standards and led the way for women around the world to succeed in the art world. She died at her summer home in St. Cloud and is buried in France.

Lesson 127
"Wool"

Write a short composition telling what you know about wool.

Use the writing and dictation worksheet at the back of this book, page 118.

Lesson 128
An Answer to a Note of Invitation

Gladys Taylor has invited Edith Morton to her birthday party next Saturday afternoon. Edith expects to go to the country on that day, to visit her cousin, and so cannot accept the invitation.

Write Edith's answer to Gladys. See letter writing rubric at the back of this book, page 114.

Extended Activity

Create an invitation to an event at your house. Include the following information. What is the event? Who is it for? What day is it? What time is it? Where is it? Make it colorful and creative.

Lesson 129
Observation Lesson

Tell—Five uses of wood. Three uses of leather. Five uses of iron. Three uses of silver. Three uses of gold. Three uses of glass. Five uses of fire. Three uses of rubber. Five uses of electricity. Some uses of water.

Use the writing and dictation worksheet at the back of this book, page 118.

Lesson 130
Reproduction—Oral and Written—"The Fox and the Stork"

Extended Activity
What lesson could we learn from this little tale? Maxims or proverbs are brief statements or mottos about life that teach us how to live. Benjamin Franklin wrote Poor Richard's Almanac that included many maxims that are good mottos to live by. He worked hard to live by these proverbs. Choose one of the following maxims and create a piece of art that represents the maxim. Be sure to write the maxim on your piece of art. A sleeping fox catches no poultry. The cat in gloves catches no mice. Little strokes fell great oaks. A penny saved is a penny earned. Eat to live and not live to eat. The worst wheel of a cart makes the most noise. God helps them that help themselves. Early to bed, early to rise, makes a man healthy, wealthy, and wise. For other maxims, see Lesson 162, page 145 in the textbook.

Lesson 131
Selection to be Memorized—"Discontent"

See the memorization rubric at the back of this book, page 108.

Lesson 132
Sentence—Statement—Question

1. Where did the buttercup grow?
2. It grew in a field.
3. A robin was resting there.

4. **What did the buttercup wish?**

5. **The buttercup wished to be a daisy.**

A group of words that expresses a thought is a *sentence*. With what kind of letter does each sentence begin?

Each sentence begins with a capital letter.

How many of the above sentences *tell* something?

Three of the sentences are telling sentences.

A sentence that tells something is a *statement*. What mark of punctuation is placed after each statement?

A period is placed after each statement.

How many of the above sentences ask something?

Two of the sentences are asking sentences.

A sentence that asks something is a *question*. What mark of punctuation is placed after a question?

A question mark is placed after a question.

Copy five sentences from your reader.

Copy five questions from your reader.

Examples may include Lessons 108 or 112.

Write five statements about the picture on page 110.

Write five questions about the picture on page 98.

Use the writing and dictation worksheet at the back of this book, page 118.

Extended Activity

Add end punctuation to the following sentences.

1. **What did you have for dinner tonight?**
2. **I had macaroni and cheese for dinner.**
3. **Did you have dessert?**
4. **Yes I had a popsicle for dessert.**
5. **What flavor was your popsicle?**
6. **It was orange.**
7. **That's my favorite dessert.**
8. **I'd eat it every meal if my mother would let me.**
9. **Why doesn't she let you?**
10. **She says it has too much sugar in it to eat three times a day.**

Lesson 133
Composition—"How Arthur Helped"

Arthur Dale was the only child of a poor widow. His mother had to work very hard to earn a living for herself and her little boy.

Arthur was ten years old. He wished very much to help his mother.

Copy these two paragraphs and finish the story, telling what Arthur did to earn some money, how much he earned, when he worked, and how the money was spent. See the essay rubric at the back of this book, page 113.

Lesson 134
Reproduction—Oral and Written— "Saint Valentine"

Extended Activity

Create a special message for someone in your life who is like Saint Valentine. Cut out a heart Thank someone who has helped you when you were sick or sad or in trouble.

Lesson 135

Observation Lesson—Oral and Written

You have watched buildings while they are being constructed; fill the following blanks, telling what these different workmen do; arrange the sentences in the order in which the work is done.

The painters
The excavators
The plumbers
The decorators
The stone masons
The lathers
The bricklayers
The plasterers
The carpenters

Possible Answers

1. **The excavators**
   The excavators dig the site where the building is to be built.
2. **The stone masons**
   The stone masons lay the foundation.
3. **The carpenters**
   The carpenters build the wooden walls.
4. **The bricklayers**
   The bricklayers lay the brick.
5. **The plumbers**
   The plumbers install the pipes for plumbing.
6. **The lathers***
   The lathers install "lathe" to which the plaster is adhered.
7. **The plasterers***
   The plasterers finish the interior walls.
8. **The painters**
   The painters apply the paint to the walls.
9. **The decorators**
   The decorators hang the pictures and arrange the furniture.

*These two steps are combined today in what is commonly called "drywall." In the past, wooden strips called lathe were attached to the wall studs with about ¼ inch spacing. On top of this, plasterers would lay a "scratch coat" of wet plaster which would squeeze into the spaces in the lathe, which "keyed" the plaster to the wall. Over this, then, the plasterers would lay on a smooth finish coat of plaster. This process, while in many ways superior to drywall, is rarely practiced today.

Lesson 136
This—That—These—Those

The words *this, that, these,* and *those* are demonstrative pronouns. We use *this* to identify an object which is near to us. Example: This is a pencil in my hand. We use *that* for an object which is further away. Example: That is his house over there. We use *these* to indicate objects which are near to us. Example: These are my toys next to me. We use *those* to indicate objects which are further away. Example: Those are his balls over there.

Copy these sentences and fill the blanks with this, that, these, those.
1. *This* tree is an elm and *that* one is a maple.
2. *These* books are mine and *those* are yours.
3. *This* flower in my hand is blue.
4. I think *those* birds have a nest in the tree.
5. *This* apple you gave me is sour.
6. Did you buy many apples like *this* one?
7. The children like to read in *these* new books.
8. *This* book I am reading is interesting.
9. *Those* horses are running away.
10. *This* knife is dull. May I borrow *that* one?

Use *this* or *that* in speaking of <u>one</u> thing. Use *these* or *those* in speaking of <u>more than one</u> thing. Use *this* or *these* in speaking of what is near. Use *that* or *those* in speaking of what is further away.

Additional practice
Complete the conversation using this, that, these, and those.

1. Could you bring me *that* basket over there?
2. I need to put *these* leaves I raked into *that* basket.
3. Do you see *that* tree next to the house?
4. *These* leaves I'm raking came from *that* tree.
5. Is *that* a glass of lemonade you're bringing me?
6. Aah, *this* is the best lemonade I've ever tasted.
7. *This* job will be finished soon now that you have helped me.
8. *Those* cold winter days are just around the corner.
9. Then *those* cold north winds will bring us snow.
10. In the spring *that* tree will sprout *those* leaves all over again.

Now write some sentences that describe things in your room using *this, that, these,* and *those*.

Lesson 137

Use these words in sentences.

1. see 2. sea 3. here 4. hear 5. by 6. buy 7. right 8. write 9. new 10. knew 11. fir 12. fur

Extended Activity

Words that sound the same but have different meanings and spellings are called homophones.

Can you think of a homophone to fit with each word below?

1. **ant**
   aunt
2. **bear**
   bare
3. **blue**
   blew
4. **cell**
   sell
5. **creak**
   creek
6. **dear**
   deer
7. **beet**
   beat
8. **heel**
   heal
9. **mail**
   male
10. **meat**
   meet
11. **plain**
   plane
12. **waist**
   waste
13. **wait**
   weight
14. **week**
   weak
15. **wood**
   would

Choose five pairs of homophones to put into sentences.

Lesson 138
Letter Writing

Denver, Colorado
Sept. 19, 1911

Dear Grace,
    Our class is going to visit the children's ward at the hospital, Saturday afternoon, and we want you to go with us. We are going to take flowers, fruit, and books to the children. Let us know if we may expect you and what you will bring.
                                    Your loving friend,
                                            Florence Bailey

Write the answer to Florence's letter. See letter writing rubric at the back of this book, page 114.

Lesson 139
Selection for Memorizing—"The Violet"

Extended Activity

Personification is a term we use to describe non-human objects that have human behaviors. Can you find one example of personification in each stanza?

Possible answers include:
    Stanza one: Dear little Violet, don't be afraid; the birds call for you; May is here waiting;
    Stanza two: why do you shiver so, Violet sweet? Violet, why peep from your earth door so silent and shy?
    Stanza three: "Ready and waiting," the slender reeds sigh. "Ready and waiting!" We sing—May and I
    Stanza four: Quick little Violet, open your eye!
    Stanza five: Hear the rain whisper, "Dear Violet, come!" Up in the pine boughs for you the winds sigh; Homesick to see you are we, May and I.
    Stanza six: Yon troop of sunbeams are winning you out.

Lesson 140

A Picture Lesson—
Feeding Her Birds

What is the name of this picture?

The name of this picture is Feeding Her Birds.

Why did the artist give it this name?

The picture resembles a mother bird feeding her little birds with open mouths who are all nestled closely together waiting to get their food.

How many little girls do you see?

You can see three little children.

Which one do you think has just been fed?

Answers may vary.

Whose turn will come next?

Answers may vary.

Write a story about the picture.

About the Artist

Jean-Francois Millet was born to a peasant family in the tiny town of Gruchy, near Cherbourg, France in 1814 to a family of Catholic Puritans. While they were poor, they valued education and as Jean-Francois grew, he read and studied Latin with the help of the priest. When he was 18, he studied in Cherbourg, under a teacher by the name of Langlois who encouraged him to go to Paris and finish his studies. As he grew older, Millet understood what poverty and need meant. He was the father of 4 sons and five daughters and struggled for the bare necessities for his family. In 1860, during a hard time in his life, he painted *Feeding Her Birds*.

The picture shows the arrangement in Millet's own home where he painted. When he was working in his studio, he often left his door open so he could hear his children at play. *Feeding Her Birds* depicts three children who have been playing in the yard, a girl of six, her younger sister, and a little brother wearing simple play clothes. While the girls' hair can be seen peeking from under their bonnets, the little boy is wearing a round cap that hides his hair. The toys scattered about are probably homemade. The older child holds a doll wrapped in a blanket. The mother has seated herself directly in front of the children, on a low milking stool which tips as she leans forward to feed the children from the long handled spoon, giving the viewer the image of a mother bird hovering over her babies.

Lesson 141

Reproduction—"The Greek Myth of Narcissus"

Read this story several times; close your book and write it.

Use the writing and dictation worksheet at the back of this book, page 118.

Lesson 142
Choice of Words

Fill these blanks with the words from the list at the end of the lesson:

1. One who writes a book is an _author_.
2. One who paints pictures is an _artist_.
3. One who draws plans for building is an _architect_.
4. A man who fights in the army is a _soldier_.
5. A _musician_ is one who makes music.
6. A _shepherd_ takes care of sheep.
7. A _poet_ writes poetry.
8. Men who sail ships are _sailors_.
9. One who studies is a _student_.
10. A _carpenter_ builds houses.
11. A _tailor_ makes men's clothes.
12. A _dressmaker_ makes ladies' clothes.
13. A _milliner_ makes ladies' hats.
14. A man who runs an engine is an _engineer_.

architect artist student milliner dressmaker poet author soldier shepherd tailor carpenter
    musician sailor engineer

Lesson 143
Observation Lesson—Oral—Foods

Possible answers.
1. **Name plants whose roots are used for food.**
   Root foods include carrots, beets, parsnips, turnips, yams, potatoes.
2. **Name plants whose stalks are used for food.**
   Stalk foods include celery and asparagus.
3. **Name plants whose leaves are used for food.**
   Leaf foods include lettuces, spinach, herbs, cabbage, Swiss chard, collard greens.
4. **Name plants whose flowers are used for food.**
   Flower foods include broccoli and cauliflower.
5. **Name plants whose seeds are used for food.**
   Seed foods include legumes such as peas, beans, peanuts, nuts from trees, sunflower seeds.
6. **What foods grow on trees?**
   Food from trees include fruits, such as avocados or oranges.

7. **What foods grow in large fields?**

   Foods in large fields include grains such as wheat and corn.

8. **What foods grow on vines?**

   Foods on vines include cucumbers, squash, melons, grapes.

9. **What foods grow in gardens?**

   Foods in gardens include all types of vegetables, berries.

10. **What foods are eaten raw?**

    Foods eaten raw are vegetables and fruits.

11. **What foods require cooking?**

    Cooked foods include meats and produce, such as eggs.

12. **From what animals do we get mutton?**

    We get mutton from sheep.

13. **From what animals do we get beef? Veal? Pork?**

    We get beef from cattle, veal from young calves, and pork from pigs.

14. **From what animals do we get venison?**

    We get venison from deer.

15. **What other animals furnish us with food?**

    Other animals that furnish food are wild game such as turkey, moose, alligator, and a large variety of fish.

Lesson 144
Letter Writing—Ralph to Harold

Ralph is going away for the summer and wants to know if Harold will take care of his pony, Rex, for him while he is gone. He will bring Rex on Saturday, if Harold's mother is willing. Write the letter for Ralph. See rubric for letter writing at the back of this book, page 114.

Lesson 145
Letter Writing—"Harold to Ralph"

Harold will be delighted to care for Rex. His mother invites Ralph to come and spend the day Saturday. Ralph can bring Rex and show Harold how a pony should be taken care of. Write the letter for Harold. See letter writing rubric at the back of this book, page 114.

Lesson 146
Conversation Lesson

If you had a piece of land on which you could plant anything you wished, What kind of shade trees would you plant? Where would you put them? What kind of shrubs would you select? What kind of fruit trees? Would you want any berry bushes? What kind? Where would you place a grape arbor? Would you want any nut trees? What kind? What kinds of flowers and vines would you have? What vegetables would you have in the garden? How would you prepare the ground for a garden? Draw a diagram, showing the best place for a house and marking places for the trees, shrubs, berry bushes and garden. Where might a hedge be placed?

Lesson 147
Selection for Memorizing—"A Boy's Song"

A good way to memorize a long poem is to identify its rhyming pattern and its repeating lines. In this poem, find and identify the words that rhyme.

Answers
> *Stanza one: deep asleep; lea me*
> *Stanza two: latest sweetest; flee me*
> *Stanza three: cleanest greenest; bee me*
> *Stanza four: steepest deepest; free me*
> *Stanza five: away play; well tell*
> *Stanza six: play hay; lea me.*

What phrases and lines are repeated?
> *The poet repeats "Where the…" in the first two lines of stanzas one to four.*
> *He repeats the line "That's the way for Billy and me" in stanzas 1-4 and stanza six.*

Lesson 148
Information Lesson—Bees

What is the home of the bees called?
> *The home of the bees is called a hive.*

How many kinds of bees are there?
> *Three—workers, drones, and queens. There are three classes of bees: the queen who lays eggs, the workers who gather food and take care of the young bees, and the drones who fertilize the queen.*

How many queens can live in each hive?

Each hive has only one queen.
What does the queen do?
The queen lays the eggs that hatch into workers.
What happens if the queen bee dies?
The workers select other larvae to feed and develop into a queen.
How do the workers keep busy?
The workers gather and carry pollen to the hive, they clean the empty cells, look after the younger bees as well as the queen, take care of the nectar and help build the comb for storing the honey.
How many sides has each cell?
Each cell has six sides.
Name two uses for these cells.
The cells may be used to store the eggs that the queen lays or they may be used to store nectar which then becomes honey.
How does a bee carry pollen?
A bee uses its hind legs to carry pollen.
What use is made of the pollen?
It may be used to feed the bees or it may be stored in the cells to be consumed later.
In what way do the bees help the flowers?
Bees help flowers by carrying pollen from the male parts or stamens of flowers to the female parts or pistils of other flowers so they can produce fruit.
How do the bees defend themselves?
Worker bees protect the hive by stinging the invaders.
What enemies have the bees?
A bee's enemies are creatures such as skunks and dragonflies that eat the bees, wax moths that eat the wax in their honeycombs, diseases that destroy the bees, and insecticides and weed sprays that destroy their food sources.

Lesson 149

Write sentences containing these words.
1. **sun**
2. **son**
3. **fore**
4. **four**
5. **flour**
6. **flower**
7. **hare**
8. **hair**

Extended Activity

In Lesson 137 you learned that words that sound the same but have different meanings and spellings are called homophones. Can you think of other pairs of homophones? Write a sentence for each pair of homophones.

Lesson 150
Reproduction—Oral and Written— "The Golden Touch"

Extended Activity

King Midas makes a wish he later regretted. Write a short story telling about a time you wished for something that turned out differently than you thought it would.

The Midas Touch is a famous reference used to describe someone who can make money easily in everything he or she does. The Midas Touch has its good and its bad sides. Complete the chart with a list of positive results and negative results of the Midas Touch. If you had the Midas Touch, how would you use it? Write a story telling how you would use the Midas Touch to benefit other people.

Positive Results	Negative Results
Wealth	Greed
One Desire Fulfilled	Other Desires Unfulfilled
Power	Lack of Control
Benefit for Self	Not a Benefit for Others

Lesson 151
Letter Writing

Write a note from Nellie Martin to Cora Arnold, asking her to go for an automobile ride next Saturday afternoon with Nellie and Nellie's Uncle Ben. Tell her that they will take their lunch with them and will not return until late.

Use the letter writing rubric at the back of this book, page 114.

Lesson 152

Write sentences containing the following words:

Answers will vary

1. see
2. saw
3. have seen or has seen
4. break
5. broke
6. have broken or has broken
7. go
8. went
9. have gone or has gone
10. draw
11. drew
12. have drawn or has drawn
13. sing
14. sang
15. have sung or has sung
16. write
17. wrote
18. have written or has written

Lesson 153

Conversation Lesson—Animals

1. **What animal is called the "king of the beasts"?**
   A lion is called the "king of beasts."
2. **Name three useful animals. Name three harmful animals.**
   Useful animals are cows for dairy products and meat, chickens for meat and eggs, pigs and sheep for meat, and small animals as pets. Harmful animals might be poisonous snakes, wild animals that are threatened, and insects such as poisonous spiders, mosquitoes and parasites.
3. **Name an animal that supplies us with warm clothing.**
   Animals that supply us with warm clothing are sheep, goats, seals and other fur-bearing animals.
4. **Name three animals that are called "beasts of burden."**
   Animals called "beasts of burden" might be oxen, donkeys, horses, mules.
5. **Name some animals that are valuable for their fur.**
   Animals valuable for their fur are sheep, goats, seals, deer, and foxes.
6. **How does a dog defend itself?**
   A dog defends itself with its bark and its bite.

7. **How does a deer defend itself?**

A deer defends itself with its fast speed, its keen sense of hearing and sight, and/or its antlers and powerful legs.

8. **How does a snake defend itself?**

A snake defends itself with its fangs or in the case of a constrictor, its powerful muscles.

9. **What is the largest animal you have seen?**

Answers will vary.

10. **What animals store away food for winter?**

Animals that store food for winter are squirrels and bears.

11. **What animal has a very long neck?**

An animal with a very long neck is a giraffe.

12. **Name an animal from which ivory is obtained.**

An elephant provides ivory.

13. **What animal cuts down trees by gnawing them with its sharp front teeth?**

A beaver cuts down trees with its front teeth.

14. **Name four kinds of fish.**

Answers will vary.

15. **Name a kind of fish that has no scales.**

Fish that have no scales are lampreys, certain kinds of eels, and catfish.

Lesson 154
Letter Writing

Write the letter which Cousin Ben sends with the package, telling the names of the plants and giving instructions about caring for them. Tell when Ben is coming to the city. See the letter writing rubric at the back of this book, page 114.

Lesson 155
Conversation Lesson—How Homes Are Lighted

How are our homes lighted?

Most American homes today are lit with electricity.

How were houses lighted many years ago?

Many years ago houses were lit with fires, candles, gas lights, or oil lamps.

How were candles made?

Candles were made with various types of hot wax including beeswax, paraffin, and tallow. The wicks were dipped repeatedly in the hot wax, or wax was poured into molds that contained a wick.

Describe a coal-oil lamp. How many parts has it? Of what use is the chimney?

Abraham Gesner introduced the coal oil lamp, known as a kerosene lamp, by refining oil from coal. It was used to light American homes in the mid to late 1800s. A kerosene lamp has three parts: the bowl containing the kerosene, the wick, and the chimney that helps to control and protect the flickering flame.

Where does gas come from?

Homes may also be lit with gas which can be both natural or manufactured from coal or petroleum. According to scientists, natural gas probably formed beneath the earth's surface many years ago.

How is it carried to a house?

When used to light homes, it may be carried to the house through pipelines, or in pressurized containers that contain LP gas, or propane, known as bottled gas.

How is gaslight put out?

Gas light is put out by turning off the gas supply.

What happens if it is blown out?

If the light is blown out, the gas may continue to seep into the air and cause an explosion.

How is electricity brought into homes?

Electricity is brought into homes through electric wires from a transformer outside the home.

How are electric lamps lighted?

Electricity is transmitted through transformers fastened to poles that support the electric wires running into homes.

How is the light put out?

Electric lights are turned off and on by light switches, which break the flow of electricity to the lights.

Lesson 156

Reproduction—Oral and Written— "The Myth of the Sunflower"

Extended Activity

Have the students draw before and after pictures of the little girl named Clytie. How does the story describe her in the beginning of the story? How did she look at the end of the story? Be sure to include the details in the story that describe colors.

Lesson 157

Selection to be Memorized—"The Sandman"

Write the first stanza of this poem from memory.

Extended Activity

What lines are repeated at the end of each stanza?

The lines repeated at the end of each stanza are Blue eyes, gray eyes, black eyes and brown, As shuts the rose, they softly close, when he goes through the town.

What color sand does the sandman use to close the babies' eyes in the first stanza?

The babies' eyes are closed with white sand in stanza one.

What color does he use to close the naughty baby's eyes in the third stanza?

The naughty baby's eyes are closed with gray sand in stanza three.

According to the second stanza, where does the sandman live?

According to the second stanza, the sandman lives on sunny beaches in another land.

What must you do when you hear the sandman's song in the fourth stanza?

When you hear the sandman's voice, "Lie softly down, dear little head, Rest quiet, busy hands."

What lines of this poem rhyme?

The poet has pairs of rhyming words in every other line except for the last two lines in each stanza when the ending words of each line rhyme.

List all the rhyming words in the four stanzas.

Stanza one: overhead, tread; down, town; crie,s eyes; hand, sand; brown, town.
Stanza two: away, day; land, sand; remote, float; way, bay; brown, town.
Stanza three: close, knows; eyes, wise; land, sand; cries, eyes; brown, town.
Stanza four: song, long; sweet, street; head, said; hands, sands; brown, town.

Lesson 158

Copy these sentences and fill the blanks with hasn't or haven't.
1. Bessie *hasn't* any new dress.
2. Tom and Frank *haven't* any ball.
3. The poor boy *hasn't* any overcoat.
4. We *haven't* seen the new pictures.
5. Will's dog *hasn't* any collar.
6. The wind *hasn't* blown today.
7. They *haven't* asked us to go.
8. I *haven't* finished my lesson.
9. My brother *hasn't* a pencil.
10. I *haven't* any pencil, either.
11. *Haven't* you a pen?
12. Jack will have to go without his lunch, for he *hasn't* any money.

Lesson 159
Birds

Answers may vary

What bird is called the "King of Birds"?

The golden eagle is called the "King of Birds."

What bird weaves its nest, hanging it in a tree?

The weaverbird weaves its nest and hangs it from a tree.

What bird pecks a hole in a tree for its nest?

A woodpecker pecks a hole in a tree for its nest.

Name three birds that are sweet singers.

Three birds that are sweet singers are canaries, wrens, and nightingales.

Name three birds that cannot sing.

Birds that cannot sing are storks, most water birds like pelicans, and birds of prey.

What bird can run as fast as a horse?

An ostrich can run as fast as a horse.

What bird makes a humming noise when it flies?

A hummingbird makes a humming noise when it flies.

Name three birds that can swim.

Birds that can swim are types of fowls like ducks and geese and seabirds like cormorants, auks, loons, terns, and pelicans.

What bird builds its nest in a chimney?

A chimney swift builds its nest in a chimney.

What bird lays its eggs in other birds' nests?

A starling lays its eggs in other birds' nests.

Name three birds that have hooked bills.

Birds that have hooked bills are birds of prey such as eagles, hawks, kites, ospreys, and falcons.

Name three birds with webbed feet.

Birds with webbed feet are ducks, geese, and swans.

What bird sleeps in the daytime?

An owl sleeps in the daytime.

Name two birds smaller than the robin.

Birds smaller than robins are wrens, sparrows, hummingbirds, nuthatches, orioles, finches, and warblers, to name a few.

Lesson 160
Letter Writing

Write Edith's reply to the letter, saying that she cannot visit her cousin this spring, and telling the reason why. She thanks Ethel for the kind invitation and hopes to be able to visit her early in the fall. Tell about the close of school and Edith's plans for the summer. See the letter writing rubric at the back of this book, page 114.

Lesson 161
A Picture Lesson—
Anxiety

What has the little girl in her hand?
Do you think she is afraid of the dog?
What would the dog say if he could talk?
Write a story about the picture.

Use the writing and dictation worksheet provided at the back of this book, page 118.

Lesson 162
For Copying and Discussion—
Maxims and Proverbs

1. We can do more good by being good than in any other way.
2. To be good is the mother of to do good.
3. The secret of being lovely is being unselfish.
4. Write on your heart that every day is the best day of the year.
5. Early to bed, early to rise, Makes a man healthy, wealthy, and wise.
6. A good beginning makes a good ending.
7. Do to others as you would that others should do to you.
8. Whatever is worth doing at all is worth doing well.
9. Where there is a will there is a way.
10. A stitch in time saves nine.

11. A good name is rather to be chosen than great riches.
12. Think before you speak.
13. A soft answer turneth away wrath.
14. Honesty is the best policy.
15. A penny saved is a penny earned.
16. Many hands make light work.

Lesson 163
Composition

Write a story illustrating one of the maxims or proverbs in Lesson 162.

Use the writing and dictation worksheet provided at the back of this book, page 118.

Lesson 164
Selection to be Memorized—
"Columbia, The Gem of the Ocean"

Extended Activity

The words to this patriotic poem were written by David T. Shaw and were set to music by Thomas
    A. Becket. Shaw describes the ship *Columbia* as the gem of the ocean. Look up the following
    words and write down their definitions. Then explain how each word adds meaning to the
    Columbia as the gem of the ocean.

shrine

definition: _____

_____

meaning added: _____

_____

devotion

definition: _____

_____

meaning added: _____

_____

homage

definition: _____

_____

meaning added: _____

_____

mandate

definition: _____

_____

meaning added: _____

_____

assemble

definition: _____

_____

meaning added: _____

_____

tyranny

definition: _____

_____

meaning added: _____

_____

desolation

definition: _____

_____

meaning added: _____

_____

deform

definition: _____

_____

meaning added: _____

_____

garlands

definition: _____

_____

meaning added: _____

_____

wither

definition: _____

_____

meaning added: _____

_____

sever

definition: _____

_____

meaning added: _____

_____

Teacher Aids

Rubrics for Student Evaluation Worksheets

Copy these aids as needed.

Memorization Rubric

Criteria	Rating Scale Not Very				Very
	1	2	3	4	5
Fluency *Reader speaks with appropriate pauses and speed.*					
Pronunciation *All words are pronounced correctly and clearly.*					
Emphasis *Appropriate emotion is used when reciting piece.*					
Memorization *Selection is memorized, and the student does not need prompting.*					
TOTAL					

Oral Presentation Rubric
Criteria

	Rating Scale				
	Not Very				Very
	1	2	3	4	5
Fluency *Reader speaks with appropriate pauses and speed.*					
Pronunciation *All words are pronounced correctly and clearly.*					
Emphasis *Appropriate emotion is used when reciting piece. The speaker does not use monotone voice.*					
TOTAL					

Composition Rubric

Criteria	Rating Scale				
	Not Very				Very
	1	2	3	4	5
Audience and Purpose *Contains an engaging introduction; main idea clearly stated.*					
Organization *Well organized, with transitions helping to link words and ideas (first, second, most important, finally, etc.).*					
Elaboration *The essay is effectively developed with specific details.*					
Use of Language *Spelling* *Varies sentence structure and makes good word choices.* *Grammar and punctuation*					
Legibility TOTAL					

Oral Reading Rubric

Criteria	Rating Scale Not Very				Very
	1	2	3	4	5
Fluency *Reader speaks with appropriate pauses and speed.*					
Pronunciation *All words are pronounced correctly and clearly.*					
Emphasis *Appropriate emotion is used when reciting piece.*					
TOTAL					

Story Rubric
Criteria

Criteria	Rating Scale Not Very				Very
	1	2	3	4	5
Focus and Directions *Student has included words and/or story line specified in the directions. Conflict and resolution is obvious..*					
Organization *Story has a beginning, middle, and end.*					
Use of Language *Spelling* *Varies sentence structure and makes good word choices.* *Grammar and punctuation*					
Legibility					
TOTAL					

Essay Rubric

Criteria	Rating Scale				
	Not Very				Very
	1	2	3	4	5
Audience and Purpose *Contains an engaging introduction; main idea clearly stated.*					
Organization *Well organized, with transitions helping to link words and ideas (first, second, most important, finally, etc.).*					
Elaboration *The essay is effectively developed with specific details.*					
Use of Language *Spelling* *Varies sentence structure and makes good word choices.* *Grammar and punctuation*					
Legibility					
TOTAL					

Letter Writing Rubric

Criteria	Rating Scale Not Very				Very
	1	2	3	4	5
Audience and Purpose *Addresses the intended audience appropriately.*					
Organization *Follows standard letter writing (greeting and salutation); uses uniform spacing; organizes information.*					
Elaboration *Clearly states and supports reasons for writing.*					
Use of Language *Uses appropriate formal language; few errors in spelling, punctuation, and grammar.*					
TOTAL					

Calendar

Envelopes

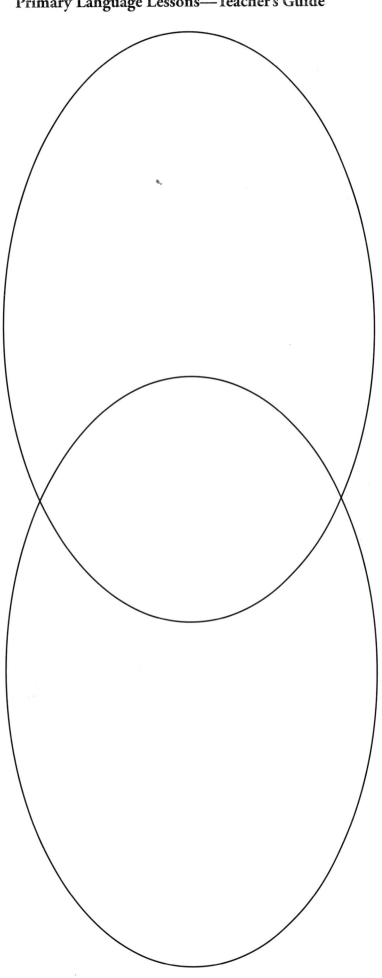

Venn Diagram

Writing and Dictation Worksheets

Books Available from
Lost Classics Book Company

American History

Stories of Great Americans for Little Americans.............................Edward Eggleston
A First Book in American History ....Edward Eggleston
A History of the United States and Its People...................................Edward Eggleston

Biography

The Life of Kit Carson.. Edward Ellis

English Grammar

Primary Language Lessons...Emma Serl
Intermediate Language Lessons ....Emma Serl
(Teacher's Guides Available for Each Reader in This Series)

Elson Readers Series

Complete Set ....William Elson, Lura Runkel, Christine Keck
The Elson Readers: Primer.. William Elson, Lura Runkel
The Elson Readers: Book One .... William Elson, Lura Runkel
The Elson Readers: Book Two .... William Elson, Lura Runkel
The Elson Readers: Book Three...William Elson
The Elson Readers: Book Four ....William Elson
The Elson Readers: Book Five .... William Elson, Christine Keck
The Elson Readers: Book Six .... William Elson, Christine Keck
The Elson Readers: Book Seven............................. William Elson, Christine Keck
The Elson Readers: Book Eight.............................. William Elson, Christine Keck
(Teacher's Guides Available for Each Reader in This Series)

Historical Fiction

With Lee in Virginia .... G. A. Henty
A Tale of the Western Plains .... G. A. Henty
The Young Carthaginian.. G. A. Henty
In the Heart of the Rockies .... G. A. Henty
For the Temple .... G. A. Henty
A Knight of the White Cross .... G. A. Henty
The Minute Boys of Lexington...Edward Stratemeyer
The Minute Boys of Bunker Hill...Edward Stratemeyer
Hope and Have .... Oliver Optic
Taken by the Enemy, First in The Blue and the Gray Series............... Oliver Optic
Within the Enemy's Lines, Second in The Blue and the Gray Series......Oliver Optic
On the Blockade, Third in The Blue and the Gray Series.........................Oliver Optic
Stand by the Union, Fourth in The Blue and the Gray Series ....Oliver Optic
Fighting for the Right, Fifth in The Blue and the Gray Series ....Oliver Optic
A Victorious Union, Sixth and Final in The Blue and the Gray Series ....Oliver Optic
Mary of Plymouth ....James Otis

For more information visit us at: http://www.lostclassicsbooks.com